SOUNDS GREAT

Intermediate Pronunciation and Speaking for Learners of English

Book 2

BEVERLY BEISBIER

Heinle & Heinle Publishers
I T P An International Thomson Publishing Company
Boston, Massachusetts 02116 U.S.A.

The publication of *Sounds Great, Book 2: Intermediate Pronunciation and Speaking for Learners of English*, was directed by the members of the Newbury House Publishing Team at Heinle & Heinle:

Erik Gundersen, Editorial Director
Martha Leibs, Production Editor
Nancy Mann, Developmental Editor
John McHugh, College ESL/EFL Market Development Director

Also participating in the publication of this program were:

Publisher: Stanley J. Galek
Editorial Production Manager: Elizabeth Holthaus
Managing Developmental Editor: Beth Kramer
Project Manager: Anita L. Raducanu/A+ Publishing Services
Assistant Editor: Karen P. Hazar
Associate Marketing Manager: Donna Hamilton
Production Assistant: Maryellen Eschmann
Manufacturing Coordinator: Mary Beth Hennebury
Illustrator: David Murray
Illustration Director: Len Shalansky
Interior Design: Robert Freese
Cover Illustrator and Designer: Bortman Design Group

Manufactured in the United States of America

Library of Congress Cataloging-in-Publication Data

Beisbier, Beverly.
    Sounds great.

    Contents: bk. 1. Beginning pronunciation for speakers
of English -- bk. 2. Intermediate pronunciation and
speaking for learners of English.
    1. English language--Pronunciation for foreign
speakers.   2. English language--Textbooks for foreign
speakers.   1. Title.
PE1157.B45 1994   428.3'4   93-41029
ISBN 0-8384-3964-0

ISBN: 0-8384-4273-0

10 9 8 7 6 5 4 3 2 1

Contents

Sounds Great is a two-level series of American English pronunciation practice materials designed for learners of English as a second or foreign language. Book One is designed for learners at the high beginning level. Book Two is geared toward intermediate-level students.

The *Sounds Great* program presents and has students practice high-frequency pronunciation points that are both central to intelligibility and challenging for most learners of English regardless of native language. The emphasis of this program is not to teach complex rules, nor is the entire range of English stress, intonation, vowel, and consonant patterns included. Rather, the two books briefly present selected pronunciation points with student rule-writing and then provide extensive hands-on practice so that students can carry key pronunciation patterns over to interaction and communication with others. The many guided conversations, pair and small group practices, information gap activities, peer interviews, and short oral reports will invite students to enjoy improving their command of spoken English.

SPECIAL FEATURES OF SOUNDS GREAT, BOOK TWO

- Awareness-building drills and ear training exercises for word stress, sentence stress, intonation, and troublesome consonants and vowels
- Activities for recognition and discovery of pronunciation and spelling rules with student-generated rule writing
- Contextualized pronunciation practice exercises graded from controlled and semi-controlled to interactive and communicative
- Student-centered pair and small group activities
- Emphasis on word stress, sentence stress, juncture, and intonation as foundations for intelligible speech
- Structures and vocabulary accessible to learners at the intermediate level
- A wide variety of topics and activity types to stimulate student interest in and enjoyment of pronunciation and speaking

ORGANIZATION OF SOUNDS GREAT, BOOK TWO

As in Book One, brief presentations, exercises, and practice activities teach learners to discover, recognize, and use American English word stress, sentence stress, juncture, intonation patterns, and high-frequency vowels and consonants. Each lesson starts with awareness-building exercises, continues to rule-writing and controlled activities, and then moves to semi-controlled and communicative interactive practice.

The first nine lessons in Book Two of this series review and expand on basic concepts of unstressed vowels, stress, juncture, and intonation presented in Book One. Additionally, learners move on to new aspects of each of these elements, such as spelling and stress correspondence, discourse focus, and categories of juncture.

Lesson 10 has learners recognize and apply intonation combinations more complex than the two basic contours. The last four lessons concentrate on a small number of high-frequency consonants and vowels that are troublesome for most learners of English regardless of native language.

THE COMPLETE SOUNDS GREAT PROGRAM

Designed to complement the student text and provide teachers and students alike with a comprehensive pronunciation program, *Sounds Great* includes the following carefully-developed components:

AUDIO PROGRAM

The *Audio Program* presents all *Intensive Practice, Pronounce Words, Pronounce Phrases, Pronounce Sentences,* and *Listening Discrimination* ear-training drills.

In the student text, the cassette symbol ( ) shows the drills, listening exercises, and examples recorded in the *Audio Program*.

The complete Tapescript is found in the *Instructor's Manual*.

INSTRUCTOR'S MANUAL

The *Instructor's Manual* offers suggested procedures for practice activities, correction and follow-up techniques, and answer keys. Appendix A provides a list of reference materials to diagnose students' pronunciation difficulties and suggested readings in the teaching of pronunciation. Appendix B classifies *Sounds Great* practice activities by grammar point, and Appendix C classifies them by topic.

Also included is the complete Tapescript of the *Audio Program*.

Acknowledgments

Inspiration from the ideas and work of John Ohala, J. Donald Bowen, and Clifford Prator have helped move me toward the completion of this textbook series, and I wish to thank them for their patient teaching and their contributions to the fields of phonology and pronunciation.

Book Two was refined through insightful comments and suggestions from the following reviewers: Scott Stevens of the University of Delaware, Karen Tucker of Georgia Institute of Technology, and Lisa Yoder of Ohio State University. It was brought into final shape with the keen eye and kind prodding of Nancy Mann at Heinle & Heinle and Anita Raducanu of A Plus Publishing Services.

I'd be remiss not to mention and thank Robert B. Kaplan, who asked a lot of thought-provoking questions that I had to address when this textbook series was conceptualized. Further appreciation goes out to pronunciation instructors at the American Language Institute of the University of Southern California who piloted parts of the material herein, especially Day Jones.

I'd also like to acknowledge the many hard-working international students who shared my enthusiasm in working through the *Sounds Great* texts.

Guide to Symbols and Figures

This symbol 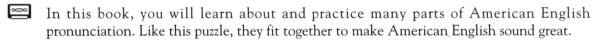 means you can listen to the *Sounds Great, Book 2*, cassette tape.

In this book, you will learn about and practice many parts of American English pronunciation. Like this puzzle, they fit together to make American English sound great.

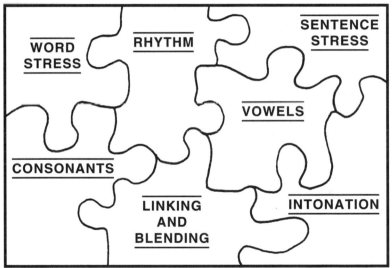

Circles and dots show stressed and unstressed syllables in words. Listen and repeat.

speaking   today   national   remember

Circles and dots also show stressed and unstressed words in sentences. Listen and repeat.

It's time to begin.   Open your book to page one.

You will see slashes and lines for rhythm groups and linking. Listen and repeat.

Here's an interesting story / to think about.

Dots and arrows show intonation. Listen and repeat.

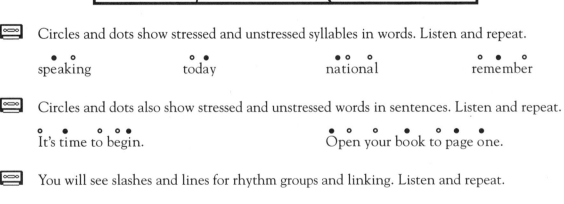

Students are sometimes busy.   Where do you live?   Are you ready?

This head shows the human organs of speech.

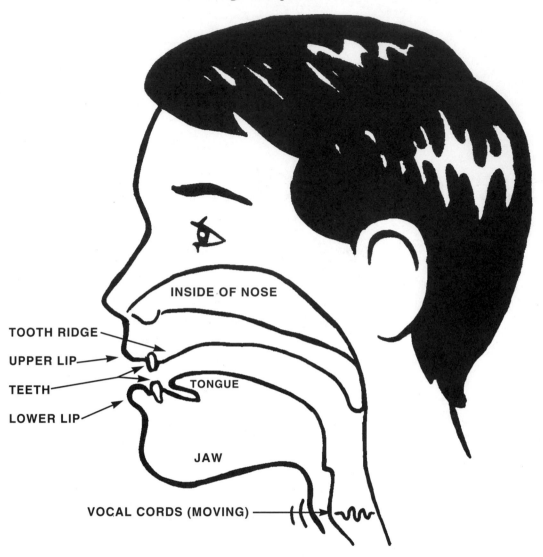

The sounds of English words are sometimes different from their spelling. Sounds are between lines like this: / /.

Sound: /iy/   Letters: <u>ea</u>sy

Sound: /z/   Letter: ro<u>s</u>e

Here are some *vowel* sounds you will practice in this book.

Listen to and repeat these vowel sounds and words.

1.	/iy/	m<u>e</u>, r<u>ea</u>d		7.	/ə/	<u>u</u>p, m<u>o</u>ther
2.	/ɪ/	<u>i</u>s, <u>i</u>t		8	/uw/	sh<u>oe</u>, m<u>oo</u>n
3.	/ɛ/	g<u>e</u>t, br<u>ea</u>d		9.	/ow/	g<u>o</u>, <u>o</u>pen
4.	/ey/	<u>ei</u>ght, b<u>a</u>by		10.	/ay/	m<u>y</u>, n<u>i</u>ght
5.	/æ/	h<u>a</u>t, <u>a</u>fter		11.	/aw/	ab<u>ou</u>t, n<u>ow</u>
6.	/a/	l<u>o</u>t, f<u>a</u>ther		12.	/ɔy/	b<u>oy</u>, j<u>oi</u>n

Do you know other words with these vowel sounds? Add them to the list. Your instructor and classmates will help you check your words.

These are shapes of lips for vowel sounds.

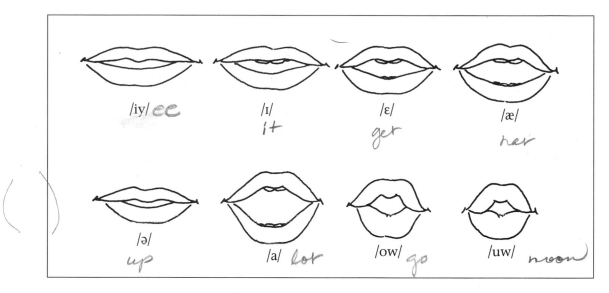

Here are some *consonant* sounds you will practice in this book.

Listen to and repeat these consonant sounds and words.

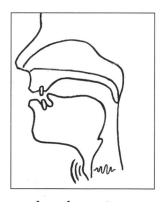

vocal cords moving

1. /b/   back, above
2. /d/   day, need
3. /g/   gold, rug
4. /v/   very, give
5. /ð/   the, this
6. /z/   zone, has
7. /dʒ/   jeans, enjoy
8. /m/   make, same
9. /n/   no, town
10. /ŋ/   sing, pink
11. /l/   look, believe
12. /r/   red, car

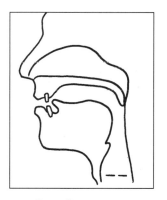

vocal cords not moving

13. /p/   pencil, drop
14. /t/   two, wait
15. /k/   candy, awake
16. /f/   find, before
17. /θ/   thin, with
18. /s/   see, city
19. /ʃ/   she, dish
20. /tʃ/   change, rich

Do you know other words with these consonant sounds? Add them to the list. Your instructor and classmates will help you check your words.

Vowels for Unstress: /ə/ and /ɪ/

PART ONE /ə/

The vowel sound /ə/ occurs many times in English words and sentences. You already know /ə/ in some common words like u̲s, th̲e̲, wa̲s, do̲es, so̲me, ju̲st, fu̲nny, mo̲nth, stu̲dy, and abo̲ve.

Contrasting the Vowels /ə/ and /a/

Many students have some problems with /ə/. /ə/ is often confused with the vowel sound /a/ (as in ho̲t, clo̲ck, fo̲llow, mo̲dern, fa̲ther).

 WARM-UP

Look at the pictures. Listen to the words and repeat them.

1. nut /ə/

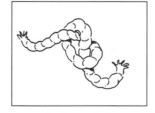

2. knot /a/

ARTICULATION

Look at the pictures. The heads and lips show how to make the sounds.

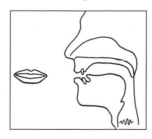

1. /ə/

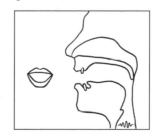

2. /a/

📼 CONTRAST

Look at the pairs of words. Listen and repeat.

shut–shot
jug–jog
fund–fond
color–collar

📼 LISTENING

Some words in English have the contrast between /ə/ and /a/. Look again at the *nut* and *knot* pictures on page 2. /ə/ is *number 1*. /a/ is *number 2*. Listen to the following words. If you hear /ə/ as in *nut*, say "one." If you hear /a/ as in *knot*, say "two."

📼 INTENSIVE PRACTICE

As a class, listen to and repeat the pairs of /ə/ and /a/ words you hear.

📼 PRONOUNCE WORDS

Listen to and repeat the /ə/ words you hear.

📼 PRONOUNCE PHRASES

Listen to and repeat the phrases you hear.

📼 PRONOUNCE SENTENCES

Listen to and repeat the sentences you hear.

PRACTICE ACTIVITIES

PARTNER 1

1a. LISTENING DISCRIMINATION AND SPEAKING. Pair Practice Words for /ə/ and /a/. PARTNER 1. Use this page. PARTNER 2. Turn to page 9.

DIRECTIONS: First, you are the speaker. Say the words to your partner. You see the vowel sound before each word. For example, you say "Number 1 is *cot*." Repeat any words your partner does not understand.

1.	/a/	cot		5.	/ə/	jug
2.	/ə/	duck		6.	/ə/	luck
3.	/ə/	rub		7.	/a/	cop
4.	/a/	stock		8.	/ə/	color

Now you are the listener. Your partner will say some words. Circle the words you hear. Ask your partner to repeat any words you do not understand. Number 9 is an example.

9.	(gut)	got		13.	bucks	box
10.	fund	fond		14.	putt	pot
11.	cup	cop		15.	run	Ron
12.	bug	bog		16.	hut	hot

Now compare answers with your partner.

2a. LISTENING DISCRIMINATION AND SPEAKING. Pair Practice Sentences for /ə/ and /a/. PARTNER 1. Use this page. PARTNER 2. Turn to page 9.

DIRECTIONS: First you are the speaker. Say the sentences to your partner. You see the vowel sound before each sentence. Repeat any sentences your partner does not understand.

1. /a/ We SHOT it.
2. /ə/ That's a nice COLOR.
3. /ə/ It was RUBBED clean.
4. /ə/ The DUCK is in the water.
5. /a/ Here's a KNOT.

Now you are the listener. Your partner will say some sentences. Circle the word you hear. Ask your partner to repeat any sentences you do not understand. Number 6 is an example.

6. I lost the _____.
   a. (bucks)   b. box

7. There's a _____ outside.
   a. bum   b. bomb

8. She's counting on her _____.
   a. luck   b. lock

9. Where are the _____?
   a. cups   b. cops

10. It's _____.
    a. stuck   b. stock

Now compare answers with your partner.

3. LISTENING DISCRIMINATION AND SPEAKING. Tick-Tack-Word. Group Game to Practice /ə/.

DIRECTIONS: Half of the class (Team 1) uses Game Board 1. The other half of the class (Team 2) uses Game Board 2. Listen to the first word. A member from each team needs to make a sentence with the word. Sentences must be longer than five words and grammatically correct. Each team that gives a correct sentence puts an X on the word with a pencil. Continue with the second word and a different team member's sentence.

EXAMPLE:
(cue) study
TEAM 1:   I never *study* for my math tests. (X on *study*)
TEAM 2:   When we *study*, we go to the library. (X on *study*)

The winners of the game are the team members who have three X's in a row down, across, or diagonally. Say TICK-TACK-WORD when you have three marks in a row.

ugly	number	discuss
instructions	comfortable	luggage
study	discover	suddenly

GAME BOARD 1

luggage	study	comfortable
discuss	ugly	instructions
suddenly	number	discover

GAME BOARD 2

4. REPORT. Class Practice for /ə/.

DIRECTIONS: Choose one of the topics. Make a three-minute report to the class about your topic.

a. Tell the class about your family. Do you have sons, daughters, brothers, or sisters? Do you have uncles and aunts with sons and daughters? How many cousins do you have?
b. Tell the class some important facts about your country's government.
c. Tell the class about an American custom or an aspect of American culture that you had trouble adjusting to.

PART TWO /ɪ/

You will need to pronounce the vowel sound /ɪ/ many times when you speak English. You already know /ɪ/ in some common words like *is*, *if*, *rich*, *thing*, *give*, *listen*, *busy*, *minute*, and *different*.

Contrasting the Vowels /ɪ/ and /iy/

Many students have some problems with /ɪ/. /ɪ/ is often confused with the vowel /iy/ (as in *eat*, *read*, *week*, *easy*, *sleepy*, and *theater*).

🔊 WARM-UP

Look at the pictures. Listen to the words and repeat them.

1. hit /ɪ/

2. heat /iy/

ARTICULATION

Look at the pictures. The heads and lips show how to make the sounds.

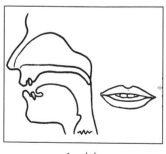

1. /ɪ/

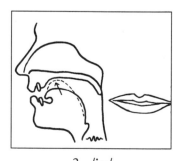

2. /iy/

CONTRAST

Look at the pairs of words. Listen and repeat.

chip – cheap
mitt – meet
pick – peek
tin – teen

LISTENING

Many words in English have the contrast between /ɪ/ and /iy/. Look again at the *hit* and *heat* pictures on page 4. /ɪ/ is *number 1*. /iy/ is *number 2*. Listen to the following words. If you hear /ɪ/ as in *hit*, say "one." If you hear /iy/ as in *heat*, say "two."

INTENSIVE PRACTICE

As a class, listen to and repeat the pairs of /ɪ/ and /iy/ words you hear.

PRONOUNCE WORDS

Listen to and repeat the /ɪ/ words you hear.

PRONOUNCE PHRASES

Listen to and repeat the phrases you hear.

PRONOUNCE SENTENCES

Listen to and repeat the sentences you hear.

PRACTICE ACTIVITIES

PARTNER 1

1a. LISTENING DISCRIMINATION AND SPEAKING. Pair Practice Words for /ɪ/ and /iy/.   PARTNER 1. Use this page. PARTNER 2. Turn to page 10.

DIRECTIONS: First, you are the speaker. Say the words to your partner. You see the vowel sound before each word. For example, you say "Number 1 is *slip*." Repeat any words your partner does not understand.

1. /ɪ/ slip
2. /ɪ/ list
3. /iy/ peach
4. /iy/ green

5. /iy/ leap
6. /iy/ each
7. /ɪ/ pick
8. /ɪ/ tin

Now you are the listener. Your partner will say some words. Circle the words you hear. Ask your partner to repeat any words you do not understand. Number 9 is an example.

9. rid (read)
10. fist feast
11. live leave
12. sit seat

13. bin bean
14. dip deep
15. rich reach
16. is ease

Now compare answers with your partner.

2a. LISTENING DISCRIMINATION AND SPEAKING. Pair Practice Sentences for /ɪ/ and /iy/. PARTNER 1. Use this page. PARTNER 2. Turn to page 10.

DIRECTIONS: First, you are the speaker. Say the sentences to your partner. You see the vowel sound before each sentence. Repeat any sentences your partner does not understand.

1. /ɪ/ We were BITTEN.
2. /iy/ She's going to LEAVE here.
3. /ɪ/ HIT them for me.
4. /ɪ/ Here's a photo of a SHIP.
5. /ɪ/ That's a good FIT.

Now you are the listener. Your partner will say some sentences. Circle the word you hear. Ask your partner to repeat any sentences you do not understand. Number 6 is an example.

6. Take a _____.
   a. (pick)   b. peek

7. This _____ is mine.
   a. mitt   b. meat

8. Where did you _____?
   a. slip   b. sleep

9. He took the _____.
   a. lid   b. lead

10. Here's the _____ I wrote.
    a. list   b. least

Now compare answers with your partner.

---

3. SPEAKING. Guided Conversations to Practice /ɪ/.

DIRECTIONS: Take turns practicing the conversations, using the lists and the example. Pronounce /ɪ/ correctly.

I. EXAMPLE:

STUDENT 1: That's a big book. What kind is it?
STUDENT 2: Mystery.
STUDENT 1: Is it interesting?
STUDENT 2: Not at all. I just can't stick with it!

KINDS OF BOOKS

business	literature	politics
fiction	mystery	religion
history	physics	statistics

II. EXAMPLE:

STUDENT 1: Did you hear about the rich widow Smith?
STUDENT 2: No, I didn't. Fill me in.
STUDENT 1: She's going to give me her mink coat!
STUDENT 2: I think you're kidding.

GIFTS

diamond ring	pink Cadillac
gold wrist watch	silver mines
import business	stock in the film industry
mink coat	symphony tickets
Picasso picture	

4. SPEAKING. Tennis Rhyme. Pair Practice Game for /ɪ/.

DIRECTIONS: You and a partner need to write your names on a piece of paper. You will also need a dictionary. Below is a word bank for the game.

PARTNER 1 says a word from the bank. This is the tennis "serve." PARTNER 2 then says a word that rhymes with the serve. Then PARTNER 1 says another word that rhymes with the serve. Continue until one partner cannot think of a rhyming word.

EXAMPLE:
PARTNER 1:   mill
PARTNER 2:   ill
PARTNER 1:   fill
PARTNER 2:   hill
PARTNER 1:   pill
PARTNER 2:   still
PARTNER 1:   kill
PARTNER 2:   I give up. You win.

The partner who continues the game longest gets one point. Then PARTNER 2 starts a new serve from the word bank. Your words must be real English words. You can check in a dictionary.

TENNIS RHYME WORD BANK
dig   kin   trip   mitt   quick   mill   slid   swim   hitch   thing

SPELLING

FIGURE IT OUT

Many one-syllable words have the sounds /ə/ or /ɪ/. Spelling helps you know when to pronounce a vowel like /ə/ or /ɪ/.

Here are some one-syllable /ə/ words. Study their spelling.

/ə/
much   sung   trust   shut   judge   club

How many vowel letters make the sound /ə/? What letter makes the sound /ə/? Write a spelling rule.

RULE FOR SPELLING /ə/

Say the sound /ə/ in a one-syllable word when the word is spelled with _____ vowel letter. The vowel letter is _____.

Exceptions:

ou		*o + e*		*others*	
touch		some	one	does	was
rough		done	none	son	the
tough		come		ton	what
young		love		won	flood
		glove		month	blood
				of	

The spelling *o* + *e* in one-syllable words is usually pronounced /ow/, as in r<u>o</u>s<u>e</u>. The single vowel letter *o* in one-syllable words is usually pronounced /a/, as in g<u>o</u>t. Look up the words *shove* and *robe* in your dictionary. Now look up *ton* and *not*. Be sure you understand the pronunciation symbols in your dictionary.

Here are some one-syllable /ɪ/ words. Study their spelling.

/ɪ/

wish   slim   lift   miss   bring   trick

How many vowel letters make the sound /ɪ/? What letter makes the sound /ɪ/? Write a spelling rule.

RULE FOR SPELLING /ɪ/

Say the sound /ɪ/ in a one-syllable word when the word is spelled with _____ vowel letter. The vowel letter is _____.

Exceptions:

g<u>i</u>v<u>e</u>   l<u>i</u>v<u>e</u>   b<u>ui</u>ld   b<u>ee</u>n   g<u>y</u>m   m<u>y</u>th

1b. LISTENING DISCRIMINATION AND SPEAKING. Pair Practice Words for /ə/ and /a/. PARTNER 2. Use this page. PARTNER 1. Turn to page 2.

DIRECTIONS: First, you are the listener. Your partner will say some words. Circle the words you hear. Ask your partner to repeat any words you do not understand. Number 1 is an example.

1.	cut	(cot)		5.	jug	jog
2.	duck	dock		6.	luck	lock
3.	rub	rob		7.	cup	cop
4.	stuck	stock		8.	color	collar

Now you are the speaker. Say the words to your partner. You see the vowel sound before each word. For example, you say "Number 9 is *gut*." Repeat any words your partner does not understand.

9.	/ə/	gut	13.	/a/	box
10.	/ə/	fund	14.	/ə/	putt
11.	/a/	cop	15.	/ə/	run
12.	/ə/	bug	16.	/a/	hot

Now compare answers with your partner.

,2b. LISTENING DISCRIMINATION AND SPEAKING. Pair Practice Sentences for /ə/ and /a/. PARTNER 2. Use this page. PARTNER 1. Turn to page 3.

DIRECTIONS: First, you are the listener. Your partner will say some sentences. Circle the word you hear. Ask your partner to repeat any sentences you do not understand. Number 1 is an example.

1. We _____ it.

   a. shut   b. (shot)

2. That's a nice _____.

   a. color   b. collar

3. It was _____ clean.

   a. rubbed   b. robbed

4. The _____ is in the water.

   a. duck   b. dock

5. Here's a _____.

   a. nut   b. knot

Now you are the speaker. Say the sentences to your partner. You see the vowel sound before each sentence. Repeat any sentences your partner does not understand.

6. /ə/   I lost the BUCKS.
7. /a/   There's a BOMB outside.
8. /ə/   She's counting on her LUCK.
9. /ə/   Where are the CUPS?
10. /a/   It's STOCK.

Now compare answers with your partner.

PAIR PRACTICE: Partner 2

1b. LISTENING DISCRIMINATION AND SPEAKING. Pair Practice Words for /ɪ/ and /iy/. PARTNER 2. Use this page. PARTNER 1. Turn to page 5.

DIRECTIONS: First, you are the listener. Your partner will say some words. Circle the words you hear. Ask your partner to repeat any words you do not understand. Number 1 is an example.

1. (slip)   sleep
2. list   least
3. pitch   peach
4. grin   green

5. lip   leap
6. itch   each
7. pick   peak
8. tin   teen

Now you are the speaker. Say the words to your partner. You see the vowel sound before each word. For example, you say "Number 9 is *read*." Repeat any words your partner does not understand.

9. /iy/   read
10. /ɪ/   fist
11. /ɪ/   live
12. /iy/   seat

13. /iy/   bean
14. /ɪ/   dip
15. /iy/   reach
16. /iy/   ease

Now compare answers with your partner.

2b. LISTENING DISCRIMINATION AND SPEAKING. Pair Practice Sentences for /ɪ/ and /iy/. PARTNER 2. Use this page. PARTNER 1. Turn to page 6.

DIRECTIONS: First, you are the listener. Your partner will say some sentences. Circle the word you hear. Ask your partner to repeat any sentences you do not understand. Number 1 is an example.

1. We were _____ .
   a. (bitten)   b. beaten
2. She's going to _____ here.
   a. live   b. leave
3. _____ them for me.
   a. Hit   b. Heat

4. Here's a photo of a _____.
   a. ship   b. sheep
5. That's a good _____.
   a. fit   b. feat

Now you are the speaker. Say the sentences to your partner. You see the vowel sound before each sentence. Repeat any sentences your partner does not understand.

6. /ɪ/   Take a PICK.
7. /iy/   This MEAT is mine.
8. /ɪ/   Where did you SLIP?

9. /iy/   He took the LEAD.
10. /ɪ/   Here's the LIST I wrote.

Now compare answers with your partner.

Word Stress and Unstress

| PART ONE | Syllables and Stress |

A **syllable** is a beat in a word. Here are some words with *one* syllable.

Listen to and repeat these words. Tap a pencil once for each word.

hear, make, you, us, book, voice, in, up, four, one, keep, stand, month, year

Most English words have two or more syllables. **Stress** means that one syllable in a word is higher, longer, and louder than other syllables in the same word.

Listen to and repeat these words with stress on the first syllable:

knowledge, sentence, possible, audience, seriously, honorable

Listen to and repeat these words with stress on the second syllable:

account, success, example, tradition, intelligent, certificate

Listen to and repeat these words with stress on the third syllable:

understand, engineer, afternoon, electronic, information, unemployment

PRACTICE ACTIVITIES

1. LISTENING DISCRIMINATION. Syllables.

DIRECTIONS: You already know many English words with *two*, *three*, or *four* syllables. Listen to these words. Circle the number of syllables you hear.

EXAMPLES:

angry   ② 3 4

difficult   2 ③ 4

1. remember 2 3 4	5. radio 2 3 4	9. special 2 3 4
2. motorcycle 2 3 4	6. necessary 2 3 4	10. technology 2 3 4
3. because 2 3 4	7. countries 2 3 4	11. everyone 2 3 4
4. important 2 3 4	8. impossible 2 3 4	12. appointment 2 3 4

2. LISTENING DISCRIMINATION AND SPEAKING. Pair Practice for Syllables.

DIRECTIONS: Write a list of twelve words. Your words need to have two, three, or four syllables. They can be in any order you wish. Read each word to a partner. Your partner will say if your words have two, three, or four syllables.

> EXAMPLE:
> YOU: wonderful
> YOUR PARTNER: Three.

3. LISTENING DISCRIMINATION. Word Stress.

DIRECTIONS: Listen to the words. Mark the stressed syllable. Blacken the dot.

> EXAMPLES: excellent   participate

1. attract
2. feature
3. useful
4. order

5. benefit
6. outstanding
7. develop
8. recommend

9. professional
10. analyzes
11. preparation
12. immediate

4. READ ALOUD.

DIRECTIONS: Now read the words above. Say the stressed syllable high, long, and loud.

5. LISTENING DISCRIMINATION.

DIRECTIONS: You will hear two words. Circle *same* if the two words have the same stressed syllable. Circle *different* if the two words do **not** have the same stressed syllable.

> EXAMPLES:
>
> result   expect   (same)   different
> emphasize   familiar   same   (different)
> authority   complicated   same   (different)

1. forget   listen   same   (different)
2. illustrate similar   (same)   different
3. daily   deny   same   (different)
4. accurate   example   same   (different)
5. technology effectiveness (same)   different
6. determine   suggestion   (same)   different
7. something   comment   (same)   different
8. community   advertisement same   (different)
9. operate   consider   same   (different)
10. environment associate   (same)   different

6a. LISTENING DISCRIMINATION AND SPEAKING. Pair Practice for Word Stress.
PARTNER 1. Use this page. PARTNER 2. Turn to page 15.

DIRECTIONS: First, you are the speaker. Read the marked words to your partner. Repeat any words your partner does not understand.

1. percent
2. manager
3. comparison
4. instant
5. relationship

6. agreement
7. members
8. atmosphere
9. competitive
10. occupation

Now you are the listener. Listen to your partner say these words. Blacken the dot of the stressed syllable. You may ask for repetition.

11. attitude
12. careless
13. experiment
14. discontinue
15. announcement

16. interview
17. recreation
18. complain
19. material
20. encourage

Now compare answers with your partner.

PART TWO   Unstress

Syllables that are low, short, and quiet are **unstressed**. Most low, short, quiet syllables in English have the vowel sound /ə/ or /ɪ/.

Listen to the unstressed syllables in these words; they sound like /ə/ as in *us*.

purpose   agree   symbol   command   seven   station   personal   condition

Listen to the unstressed syllables in these words; they sound like /ɪ/ as in *it*.

music   belong   credit   report   pilot   discuss   imagine   mechanic   elected

Unstressed syllables are spelled with many different vowel letters. Their spelling does not change their unstressed pronunciation /ə/ or /ɪ/.

PRACTICE ACTIVITIES

1. READ ALOUD.

DIRECTIONS: Read the following sentences aloud. Pronounce the underlined, unstressed vowels like /ə/.

1. There's a long-distance call from your parents.
2. I have a question about your proposal.
3. The school will admit seven hundred students.
4. The president happens to be a woman.
5. A famous actress read the welcome statement.

Pronounce the underlined, unstressed vowels like /ɪ/.

6. The off<u>ices</u> are d<u>i</u>rectl<u>y</u> oppos<u>i</u>te room <u>e</u>lev<u>e</u>n.
7. My <u>e</u>xperiment didn't have <u>e</u>xact stat<u>i</u>st<u>i</u>cs.
8. She r<u>e</u>viewed a compl<u>i</u>cat<u>e</u>d r<u>e</u>port on coll<u>e</u>ges.
9. A knowl<u>e</u>dgeable scient<u>i</u>st <u>i</u>nvent<u>e</u>d this <u>i</u>nstrument.
10. He <u>e</u>xpect<u>e</u>d to r<u>e</u>ceive an A on the bus<u>i</u>n<u>e</u>ss <u>e</u>xam.

PARTNER 1

2a. LISTENING DISCRIMINATION AND SPEAKING. Pair Practice for Word Stress and Unstress.   PARTNER 1. Use this page. PARTNER 2. Turn to page 16.

DIRECTIONS: First, you are the speaker. Say the pairs of words to your partner. Pronounce the stressed syllables high, long, and loud. Pronounce the syllable without stress like /ə/ or /ɪ/. Some pairs of words have the same stress pattern and some do not. Your partner will circle *same* or *different*. Repeat any words your partner does not understand.

EXAMPLES:

a. permanent   b. detective   same   (different)

a. national   b. confidence   (same)   different

1. a. practical   b. expensive   (*different*)

2. a. diploma   b. examine   (*same*)

3. a. majority   b. intelligent   (*same*)

4. a. solution   b. vitamin   (*different*)

5. a. television   b. imitation   (*different*)

Now you are the listener. Your partner will say some words. Circle *same* if the two words have the same stress pattern. Circle *different* if the two words have a different stress pattern. Ask your partner to repeat any words you do not understand.

6. a. disagree   b. suggested   same   different

7. a. usefulness   b. typical   same   different

8. a. equipment   b. confusing   same   different

9. a. responsible   b. innovative   same   different

10. a. appointment   b. imagine   same   different

Now compare answers with your partner.

PART THREE

Stress in Dictionaries

When you learn vocabulary as you read, you do not hear stress. English speakers use word stress to understand what you say, so correct word stress is important. If you need to know stress of new words, you can look in a dictionary.

Look up the three-syllable word *confident* in your dictionary. Is it clear which syllable has stress? Look up the four-syllable word *executive* in your dictionary. Is it clear which syllable has stress? If you do not understand how your dictionary shows stress, ask your instructor.

In Lessons 3, 4, and 5, you will learn how to find stress in many words without using a dictionary!

PARTNER 2

6b. LISTENING DISCRIMINATION AND SPEAKING. Pair Practice for Word Stress.
PARTNER 2. Use this page. PARTNER 1. Turn to page 13.

DIRECTIONS: First, you are the listener. Listen to your partner say these words. Blacken the dot of the stressed syllable. You may ask for repetition.

1. percent
2. manager
3. comparison
4. instant
5. relationship

6. agreement
7. members
8. atmosphere
9. competitive
10. occupation

Now you are the speaker. Read the marked words to your partner. Repeat any words your partner does not understand.

11. attitude
12. careless
13. experiment
14. discontinue
15. announcement

16. interview
17. recreation
18. complain
19. material
20. encourage

Now compare answers with your partner.

PAIR PRACTICE: Partner 2

2b. LISTENING DISCRIMINATION AND SPEAKING. Pair Practice for Word Stress and Unstress. PARTNER 2. Use this page. PARTNER 1. Turn to page 14.

DIRECTIONS: First, you are the listener. Your partner will say some words. Circle *same* if the two words have the same stress pattern. Circle *different* if the two words have a different stress pattern. Ask your partner to repeat any words you do not understand.

EXAMPLES:

    a. permanent   b. detective   *same* (*different*)

    a. national   b. confidence   (*same*) *different*

1. a. practical   b. expensive   *same*   *different*

2. a. diploma   b. examine   *same*   *different*

3. a. majority   b. intelligent   *same*   *different*

4. a. solution   b. vitamin   *same*   *different*

5. a. television   b. imitation   *same*   *different*

Now you are the speaker. Say the pairs of words to your partner. Pronounce the stressed syllable high, long, and loud. Pronounce the syllable without stress like /ə/ or /ɪ/. Some pairs of words have a different stress pattern. Your partner will circle *same* or *different*. Repeat any words your partner does not understand.

6. a. disagree   b. suggested   (*different*)

7. a. usefulness   b. typical   (*same*)

8. a. equipment   b. confusing   (*same*)

9. a. responsible   b. innovative   (*different*)

10. a. appointment   b. imagine   (*same*)

Now compare answers with your partner.

Word Stress and Spelling Patterns

PART ONE ## Pairs Spelled Alike

Here are some nouns and verbs spelled the same. You see some adjectives and verbs spelled the same, too. Read and listen to these examples:

NOUNS
I need a *hammer*.
Here's my *report*.
He made a fast *escape*.
What *color* do you like?
We have an *interview* on Monday.

VERBS
Hammer this nail.
He will *report* the news.
The prisoner can't *escape*.
Color the tree brown and green.
They might *interview* you soon.

ADJECTIVES
This is a *direct* road to town.
A *major* accident occurred last night.
I was *alert* and ready.
The bag was *empty*.
We rode an *express* train.

VERBS
Lee *directed* the visitors to the lobby.
He's *majoring* in history.
A signal will *alert* you to stop.
Empty your pockets.
She *expresses* her ideas well.

FIGURE IT OUT

Listen to the words spelled alike. Blacken the dot over the stressed syllable.

EXAMPLE: cover cover

1. surprise surprise
2. circle circle
X 3. delay delay
4. promise promise

5. forward forward
X 6. diet diet
7. exercise exercise
8. deposit deposit

Now write a rule.

RULE FOR WORDS SPELLED ALIKE

For most pairs of words spelled alike, the stress *(circle one)* changes   does not change.

Exceptions:

In a small group of word pairs, stress changes. These changes are not predictable by spelling.

Listen to and repeat these examples:

NOUNS	VERBS	NOUNS	VERBS	NOUNS	VERBS
combat	combat	export	export	progress	progress
conduct	conduct	import	import	project	project
conflict	conflict	increase	increase	protest	protest
contest	contest	insult	insult	record	record
contract	contract	object	object	refund	refund
contrast	contrast	permit	permit	subject	subject
convict	convict	present	present	survey	survey
digest	digest	produce	produce	suspect	suspect

PRACTICE ACTIVITY

PARTNER 1

LISTENING DISCRIMINATION AND SPEAKING. Pair Practice for Stress Change.
PARTNER 1. Use this page. PARTNER 2. Turn to page 23.

DIRECTIONS: First, you are the speaker. Say each word. Stress is marked. Your partner will say "noun" or "verb." If your partner does not answer correctly, repeat the word.

EXAMPLE:

YOU: suspect
YOUR PARTNER: verb
YOU: That's right.

1. record (noun)   3. contrast (verb)   5. combat (noun)
2. object (verb)   4. import (noun)

Now you are the listener. Your partner will say one of the two words. Circle the *one* word you hear. Then say "noun" or "verb."

EXAMPLE:

YOUR PARTNER: suspect
YOU: verb
YOUR PARTNER: That's right.

6. a. permit (noun)   b. permit (verb)   9. a. digest (noun)   b. digest (verb)
7. a. increase (noun) b. increase (verb)   10. a. contest (noun)   b. contest (verb)
8. a. present (noun)   b. present (verb)

PART TWO

Verbs Ending in Two Consonants

FIGURE IT OUT

Most verbs spelled with two consonant letters at the end have the same stress pattern. Listen to the words. Blacken the dot over the stressed syllable.

EXAMPLES: invent   arrest

1. collect
2. assign
3. enroll
4. defend
5. understand
6. interrupt
7. disappoint
8. represent

Which syllable of verbs ending in two consonants has stress? Write a rule.

RULE FOR VERBS ENDING IN TWO CONSONANTS

In most verbs ending in two consonants, the _____ syllable has stress.

Exceptions: Verbs ending in *-ish* (*finish, polish, distinguish*) are exceptions to this rule. Listen to these other exceptions to the rule. Which syllable is stressed?

comment   interest   experiment

PRACTICE ACTIVITIES

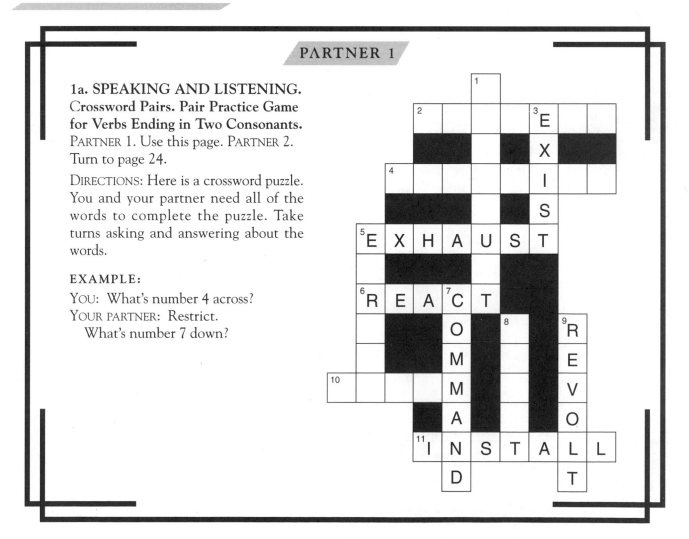

PARTNER 1

1a. SPEAKING AND LISTENING. Crossword Pairs. Pair Practice Game for Verbs Ending in Two Consonants. PARTNER 1. Use this page. PARTNER 2. Turn to page 24.

DIRECTIONS: Here is a crossword puzzle. You and your partner need all of the words to complete the puzzle. Take turns asking and answering about the words.

EXAMPLE:

YOU: What's number 4 across?
YOUR PARTNER: Restrict.
    What's number 7 down?

2a. LISTENING DISCRIMINATION AND SPEAKING. Pair Practice for Verbs Ending in Two Consonants. PARTNER 1. Use this page. PARTNER 2. Turn to page 25.

DIRECTIONS: First, you are the speaker. Say each sentence and question to your partner. Stress the verb ending in two consonants correctly. Your partner will create an answer with the same verb.

EXAMPLE:

YOU: I missed our last class. What homework did the instructor collect?
YOUR PARTNER: He collected the vocabulary exercises.

1. I'd like to see a good movie. What do you recommend?
2. I've just changed my phone number. Who do I need to inform?
3. Our class needs a president. Who should we elect?
4. My English isn't getting better. How can I progress?
5. I left our last class early. What homework did the instructor assign?

Now you are the listener. Your partner will say a sentence and ask you a question. Use the verb in the question to create your own answer.

EXAMPLE:

YOUR PARTNER: I missed our last class. What homework did the instructor collect?
YOU: She didn't collect any homework.

PART THREE Words Ending in Two Consonants + *-ive*

FIGURE IT OUT

Words spelled with two consonant letters + *-ive* at the end have the same stress pattern. Listen to the words. Blacken the dot over the stressed syllable.

EXAMPLES:

constructive   progressive

1. inventive   5. inexpensive
2. distinctive   6. unattractive
3. impressive   7. ineffective
4. descriptive   8. unresponsive

Which syllable of words ending in two consonants + *-ive* has stress? Write a rule.

RULE FOR WORDS ENDING IN TWO CONSONANTS + *-IVE*

In words ending in two consonants + *ive,* the syllable _____ *-ive* has stress.

Exception: Listen to this exception to the rule. Which syllable is stressed?

adjective

PARTNER 1

1a. LISTENING DISCRIMINATION AND SPEAKING. Pair Practice for Words Ending in Two Consonants + *-ive*. PARTNER 1. Use this page. PARTNER 2. Turn to page 25.

DIRECTIONS: Make these statements to your partner. Listen to your partner's response. If your partner does not respond correctly, repeat the statements.

EXAMPLE:

YOU: Joe is a bad student. He interrupts the teacher.
YOUR PARTNER: You're right. He's interruptive.

1. Tammy's a good actress. She expresses herself well.
2. Hurricanes can be terrible. They destroy things.
3. This is a beautiful painting! I'm impressed!
4. I can't afford this car. It costs too much money.
5. Mike is a good student. He pays attention in class.

Now your partner will make some statements. Choose a response from the phrase bank. Stress the words correctly. If you do not respond correctly, your partner will repeat the statements.

PHRASE BANK

Yes, she's attractive.
I know. He's disruptive.
You're right. It's instructive.
That's true. He was very inventive.
I agree. It's offensive.

2. DISCUSS AND REPORT. Small Group Practice for Words Ending in Two Consonants + *-ive*.

DIRECTIONS: You and your group need to choose one of the topics. Discuss the topic with your group. Then tell the class the results of your discussion.

a. Here is a list of five personal qualities. Which one is the most important quality in a friend? Why? Which one is the least important quality in a friend? Why?

inventive, supportive, perceptive, attentive, impressive

b. Here is a list of adjectives. Which one describes a good parent? Why? Which one describes a bad parent? Why?

permissive, restrictive, protective, progressive, receptive

c. Here is a list of five personal qualities. Which one is the most important in a spouse or boyfriend/girlfriend? Why? Which one is the least important in a spouse or boyfriend/girlfriend? Why?

responsive, assertive, attractive, possessive, supportive

PART FOUR

Verbs Ending in -*ate*

FIGURE IT OUT

Three- and four-syllable verbs spelled with -*ate* at the end have the same stress pattern.

 Listen to these examples. Blacken the dot over the stressed syllable.

EXAMPLES:

● o o   o   ● o o
regulate   appreciate

1. o o o   5. o o o o
   illustrate   refrigerate

2. o o o   6. oo o o
   calculate   cooperate

3. o oo   7. o o o o
   graduate   investigate

4. o o o   8. o o oo
   decorate   negotiate

Which syllable of three- and four-syllable verbs ending in -*ate* has stress? Write two rules.

RULES FOR VERBS ENDING IN -*ATE*

1. In three-syllable verbs ending in -*ate*, the _____ syllable has stress.
2. In four-syllable verbs ending in -*ate*, the _____ syllable has stress.

PRACTICE ACTIVITIES

1. SPEAKING. Guided Conversation to Practice Verbs Ending in -*ate*.
DIRECTIONS: Take turns practicing the conversation, using the list of Joe's talents and the model. Stress verbs ending in -*ate* correctly.

EXAMPLE:

STUDENT 1:   Joe fascinates me. I appreciate his talent.
STUDENT 2:   I'm not sure what you mean.
STUDENT 1:   He's always able to <u>calculate difficult problems</u>.
STUDENT 2:   Oh, come on. Don't exaggerate!

JOE'S TALENTS

negotiate contracts   participate in discussions
motivate his fellow workers   speculate on good investments
calculate difficult problems   anticipate new trends
communicate his ideas   operate new computer programs
demonstrate goodwill   concentrate on his work
cooperate with his boss   investigate good business deals

MODEL CONVERSATION

STUDENT 1:   Joe fascinates me. I appreciate his talent.
STUDENT 2:   I'm not sure what you mean.
STUDENT 1:   He's always able to _____.
STUDENT 2:   Oh, come on. Don't exaggerate!

2. INTERVIEW. Birthdays and Parties. Pair Practice for Verbs Ending in *-ate*.

DIRECTIONS: Interview a partner. Use the questions below. You can take notes to remember your partner's answers. Your partner will interview you, too. Choose who will ask or answer first. After the interviews, tell the other students in the class about your partner. You can use your notes. When you speak to the class about your partner, stress your words correctly.

BIRTHDAYS

1. How do you celebrate your birthday?
2. What kind of presents do you appreciate getting?
3. What kind of present would you hesitate to give a friend you don't know very well?

PARTIES

1. Do you circulate at parties?
2. Do you initiate conversations at parties?
3. How do you indicate to the host of a party that you are going to leave?

PARTNER 2

LISTENING DISCRIMINATION AND SPEAKING. Pair Practice for Stress Change.
PARTNER 2. Use this page. PARTNER 1. Turn to page 18.

DIRECTIONS: First, you are the listener. Your partner will say one of the two words. Circle the *one* word you hear. Then say "noun" or "verb."

EXAMPLE:

YOUR PARTNER: suspect
YOU: verb
YOUR PARTNER: That's right.

1. a. record (noun)   b. record (verb)   4. a. import (noun)   b. import (verb)
2. a. object (noun)   b. object (verb)   5. a. combat (noun)   b. combat (verb)
3. a. contrast (noun) b. contrast (verb)

Now you are the speaker. Say each word. Stress is marked. Your partner will say "noun" or "verb." If your partner does not answer correctly, repeat the word.

EXAMPLE:

YOU: suspect
YOUR PARTNER: verb
YOU: That's right.

6. permit (verb)   8. present (verb)   10. contest (noun)

7. increase (noun)   9. digest (verb)

1b. SPEAKING AND LISTENING. Crossword Pairs. Pair Practice Game for Verbs Ending in Two Consonants. PARTNER 2. Use this page. PARTNER 1. Turn to page 19.

DIRECTIONS: Here is a crossword puzzle. You and your partner need all of the words to complete the puzzle. Take turns asking and answering about the words.

EXAMPLE:

YOU: What's number 7 down?

YOUR PARTNER: Command. What's number 4 across?

2b. LISTENING DISCRIMINATION AND SPEAKING. Pair Practice for Verbs Ending in Two Consonants.   PARTNER 2. Use this page. PARTNER 1. Turn to page 20.

DIRECTIONS: First, you are the listener. Your partner will say a sentence and ask you a question. Use the verb in the question to create your own answer.

EXAMPLE:

YOUR PARTNER: I missed our last class. What homework did the instructor collect?
YOU: He collected the vocabulary exercises.

Now you are the speaker. Say each sentence and question to your partner. Stress the verb ending in two consonants correctly. Your partner will create an answer with the same verb.

EXAMPLE:

YOU: I missed our last class. What homework did the instructor collect?
YOUR PARTNER: She didn't collect any homework.

6. I'd like to take a good class. What class should I select?
7. Our class needs a secretary. Who should we appoint?
8. Here are the letters A-S-A-P. What do they represent?
9. I want to buy a good car. What kind do you suggest?
10. I'm going to study here next term. How soon can I enroll?

PARTNER 2

1b. LISTENING DISCRIMINATION AND SPEAKING. Pair Practice for Words Ending in Two Consonants + -ive.   PARTNER 2. Use this page. PARTNER 1. Turn to page 21.

DIRECTIONS: First, your partner will make some statements. Choose a response from the phrase bank. Stress the words correctly. If you do not respond correctly, your partner will repeat the statements.

EXAMPLE:

YOUR PARTNER: Joe is a bad student. He interrupts the teacher.
YOU: You're right. He's interruptive.

PHRASE BANK
That's true. He's attentive.
You're right. They're destructive.
I know. It's expensive.
I agree. She's expressive.
Oh, yes. It's impressive.

Now make these statements to your partner. Listen to your partner's response.

If your partner does not respond correctly, repeat the statements.

6. I don't watch that TV show. It offends me.
7. I liked this book. I learned a lot from it.
8. Sam's a bad student. He disrupts the class.
9. Edison was an intelligent man. He invented a lot of machines.
10. Amanda is a nice girl. She's very pretty, too.

PAIR PRACTICE: Partner 2

Predictable Word Stress with Suffixes

PART ONE Words Ending in *-ion, -ic,* and *-ics*

 FIGURE IT OUT

Listen to these words ending in *-ion, -ic,* and *-ics.* Blacken the dot over the stressed syllable.

EXAMPLES:

fraction   domestic

1. session
2. nation
3. opinion
4. exception
5. profession
6. motivation
7. combination
8. introduction
9. examination
10. pronunciation

11. metric
12. physics
13. plastic
14. artistic
15. magnetic
16. italics
17. statistics
18. academic
19. problematic
20. economics

Now write a rule.

RULE FOR WORDS ENDING IN *-ION, -IC,* AND *-ICS*

For words ending in *-ion, -ic,* and *-ics,* stress the syllable _____ *-ion, -ic,* or *-ics.*

 Exceptions: Listen to these exceptions to the rule. Which syllable is stressed?

television   lunatic   politics   Catholic   arithmetic

1. SPEAKING. Pair or Group Practice for Words Ending in *-ion, -ic,* and *-ics*.
DIRECTIONS: Here are grade reports of four Mission Polytechnic students. Take turns asking and answering questions about the courses they took last year. Stress *-ion, -ic,* and *-ics* words correctly.

EXAMPLE:
STUDENT 1:   When did Penny Bastion take Applied Mathematics?
STUDENT 2:   The Winter Quarter. What courses did Su-An Chang take during the Spring Quarter?
STUDENT 3:   Robotics, Electronic Circuits, and Gymnastics. Who took Laboratory Operations?
STUDENT 4:   Stanley Killion. What grade did Gary Williams get in Hispanic Language and Culture?

MISSION POLYTECHNIC
Grade Report
STUDENT: Stanley Killion

Fall Quarter

Introduction to Biology	A
Music Appreciation	C
World Religions	B

Winter Quarter

Organic Chemistry	A
Scientific Methods	A
Athletics	C

Spring Quarter

Genetics	B
Laboratory Operations	A
Dramatic Arts	B

MISSION POLYTECHNIC
Grade Report
STUDENT: Penny Bastion

Fall Quarter

Statistics	A
American Institutions	B
English Composition	B

Winter Quarter

Applied Mathematics	A
Ceramics	C
Microcomputer Applications	A

Spring Quarter

Introduction to Physics	B
Aerobics	A
Foundations of Calculus	A

MISSION POLYTECHNIC
Grade Report
STUDENT: Gary Williams

Fall Quarter

Introduction to Linguistics	A
U.S. Government and Politics	C
Classics in Translation	C

Winter Quarter

Semantics	A
Hispanic Language and Culture	B
Physical Education	A

Spring Quarter

Speech and Communication	B
Oceanic Languages	C
Spanish Conversation	B

MISSION POLYTECHNIC
Grade Report
STUDENT: Su-An Chang

Fall Quarter

Introduction to Algebra	B
Nutrition	B
Telecommunications	A

Winter Quarter

Symbolic Logic	B
Economics	B
Harmonics and Acoustics	A

Spring Quarter

Robotics	A
Electronic Circuits	A
Gymnastics	A

2a. LISTENING DISCRIMINATION AND SPEAKING. Pair Practice for Stress on -ion, -ic, and -ics Words. PARTNER 1. Use this page. PARTNER 2. Turn to page 32.

DIRECTIONS: Ask your partner these questions. Listen to your partner's answer. If your partner does not answer correctly, repeat the questions.

Questions	Answer
1. What class did you take in high school?	(Mathematics.)
2. Is your morning class a lecture course?	(No. Discussion.)
3. What kind of government does the U.S. have?	(Democrátic.)
4. What do you call money paid to take classes?	(Tuition.)
5. How would you describe the movie you saw?	(Fantastic!)
6. What does *quote* mean?	(Quotation.)

Now your partner will ask some questions. Choose an answer from the answer bank. Stress the words correctly. If you do not answer correctly, your partner will repeat the questions.

ANSWER BANK

Conversation.	No. Domestic.	The Pacific.
Definitions.	Education.	Traffic.

3. DISCUSS AND REPORT. Modernization. Small Class or Group Activity to Practice Words Ending in -ion, -ic, and -ics.

Modernization sometimes makes our lives better. However, it also can bring new problems into our lives.

DIRECTIONS: You and your group should choose *one* of the topics below. First, discuss two ways modernization has made your topic area better. Then, discuss two problems of modernization for your topic area. Finally, tell the class the four main points of your discussion.

a. transportation
b. communication
c. population distribution

d. economic growth
e. education and academic opportunities
f. food, diet, and nutrition

PART TWO Words Ending in -ial, -ical, and -ity

☞ FIGURE IT OUT

Listen to these words ending in -ial, -ical, and -ity. Blacken the dot over the stressed syllable.

EXAMPLES: special typical

1. social
2. partial
3. official
4. material
5. industrial
6. presidential

7. influential
8. confidential
9. logical
10. vertical
11. medical
12. identical

13. grammatical
14. historical
15. alphabetical
16. theoretical
17. quantity
18. gravity

19. ability
20. security
21. necessity
22. generosity
23. opportunity

Now write a rule.

RULE FOR WORDS ENDING IN -IAL, -ICAL, AND -ITY

For words ending in *-ial, -ical,* and *-ity,* stress the syllable _____ *-ial, -ical,* or *-ity.*

PRACTICE ACTIVITIES

PARTNER 1

1a. LISTENING DISCRIMINATION AND SPEAKING. Pair Practice for Stress on *-ial, -ical,* and *-ity* Words.   PARTNER 1. Use this page. PARTNER 2. Turn to page 32.

DIRECTIONS: Ask your partner these questions. Listen to your partner's answer. If your partner does not answer correctly, repeat the questions.

Questions

1. What's the opposite of *horizontal?*
2. What word means the same as *speed?*
3. What do you call an advertisement on TV?
4. What's the opposite of *whole?*
5. What's organization in order from 1 to 100?
6. What's the opposite of *fantasy?*
7. What word means the same as *inexpensive?*
8. What's the opposite of *informality?*

Answer

(Vertical.)
(Velocity.)
(A commercial.)
(Partial.)
(Numerical.)
(Reality.)
(Economical.)
(Formality.)

Now your partner will ask some questions. Choose an answer from the answer bank. Stress the words correctly. If you do not answer correctly, your partner will repeat the questions.

ANSWER BANK

Alphabetical.	Comical.	Identical.	Special.
A celebrity.	Complexity.	Security.	A university.

2. INTERVIEW. Astrological Personalities. Pair Practice for Words Ending in *-ial, -ical,* and *-ity.*

DIRECTIONS: Signs of the zodiac, birth dates, and descriptions of personalities are on page 30. Ask and answer questions about the personalities. Try to figure out which sign of the zodiac your partner is. Stress *-ial, -ical,* and *-ity* words correctly.

EXAMPLE:

STUDENT 1:   Do you enjoy doing things beneficial for humanity?
STUDENT 2:   Yes, I do.
STUDENT 1:   Do you like classical poetry and theoretical ideas?
STUDENT 2:   Not really.
STUDENT 1:   I don't think you're a Pisces.
STUDENT 2:   You're right. I'm not a Pisces.

When your interviews are finished, tell the class about your partner's sign of the zodiac and personality.

Aquarius Jan. 20–Feb. 18

Aquarians are cordial and full of curiosity and originality. They sometimes express controversial and radical ideas. Their sensitivity can make others hurt them easily. They have a special ability in reading people's character. They find compatibility with Leos.

 Pisces Feb. 19–Mar. 20

Pisceans are patient and enjoy doing things beneficial for humanity. They like both classical poetry and theoretical ideas. They have the ability to go from one extreme to another. They like to tackle impossibilities. They find compatibility with Virgos.

 Aries Mar. 21–Apr. 19

Aries are full of energy and spontaneity. They are independent and do not look for security in others. They love variety and diversity. Encouragement from others is influential and sometimes essential. They find compatibility with Librans.

 Taurus Apr. 20–May 20

Taureans are practical. They like stability and uniformity. They are reserved and full of dignity. They are determined and logical in reaching their goals. They love friendships with sincerity, and affection from others is essential. They find compatibility with Scorpios.

Gemini May 21–June 20

Geminis are charming and full of sensitivity and flexibility. They like material things. They have the special capacity to show the good side of their personalities. Others are not critical of them. They find compatibility with Sagittarians.

Cancer June 21–July 22

Cancers have creativity, originality, and imagination. They like familial stability and are sympathetic. A typical Cancer has substantial memory for details. They enjoy productivity and always try to do their best. They find compatibility with Capricorns.

 Leo July 23–Aug. 22

Leos are very social and full of vanity. They can be influential political leaders because they excel in authority and managerial skill. They love life and their flexibility helps them easily recover from difficulties. They find compatibility with Aquarians.

 Virgo Aug. 23–Sept. 22

Virgos are analytical and sometimes lack spontaneity. They have a practical ability for organization. They are true, beneficial friends. They are full of charity and enjoy helping others. They find compatibility with Pisceans.

 Libra Sept. 23–Oct. 22

Libras are full of creativity and curiosity. They have a thoughtful mentality. They like equality and enjoy symmetrical balance in their lives. They are idealistic and sometimes illogical. They find compatibility with Aries.

 Scorpio Oct. 23–Nov. 21

Scorpios have influential, magnetic personalities. They try to reach their goals with intensity. Sometimes they are jealous of others. They do not like to talk about confidential things. They enjoy finding answers to mystical and magical problems. They find compatibility with Taureans.

 Sagittarius Nov. 22–Dec. 21

Sagittarians are social and being with others is a necessity. They like variety and adventure. They are full of sincerity. Hard work is essential for them. They are never superficial in reaching their goals. They find compatibility with Geminis.

 Capricorn Dec. 22–Jan. 19

Capricorns are practical and full of sensibility. Hard work is critical for them. They show maturity and discipline in their activities. They excel in positions of responsibility and enjoy having others rely on their capability. They find compatibility with Cancers.

3. DISCUSS AND REPORT. Small Class or Group Activity to Practice Words Ending in *-ial*, *-ical*, and *-ity*.

DIRECTIONS: You and your group should choose one of the topics below. Discuss three qualities that you believe are most important for your topic. Then discuss why your three qualities are important. Finally, tell the class the results of your discussion.

Topics	Qualities
an economical car	creativity
a theatrical performance	utility
a presidential candidate	dependability
a television commercial	authority
an official document	clarity
a medical examination	originality
	sincerity
	simplicity
	popularity
	security
	formality
	visibility
	availability

PAIR PRACTICE: Partner 2

PARTNER 2

**2b. LISTENING DISCRIMINATION AND SPEAKING. Pair Practice for Stress on
-ion, -ic, and -ics Words.**   PARTNER 2. Use this page. PARTNER 1. Turn to page 28.

DIRECTIONS: First, your partner will ask some questions. Choose an answer from the answer bank.
Stress the words correctly. If you do not answer correctly, your partner will repeat the questions.

ANSWER BANK

Democratic.	Fantastic!	Quotation.
No. Discussion.	Mathematics.	Tuition.

Now ask your partner these questions. Listen to your partner's answer. If your partner does not
answer correctly, repeat the questions.

Questions   *Answers*

7. Do you drive a foreign car?   (No. Domestic.)
8. What's the main reason people go to school?   (Education.)
9. Why were you late for class today?   (Traffic.)
10. What do we call talk between people?   (Conversation.)
11. What ocean is on the West Coast of the U.S.?   (The Pacific.)
12. What can you find in a dictionary?   (Definitions.)

PARTNER 2

**1b. LISTENING DISCRIMINATION AND SPEAKING. Pair Practice for Stress on
-ion, -ic, and -ics Words.**   PARTNER 2. Use this page. PARTNER 1. Turn to page 29.

DIRECTIONS: First your partner will ask some questions. Choose an answer from the answer
bank. Stress the words correctly. If you do not answer correctly, your partner will repeat the
questions.

ANSWER BANK

A commercial.	Numerical.	Vertical.
Economical.	Partial.	Velocity.
Formality.	Reality.	

Now ask your partner these questions. Listen to your partner's answer. If your partner does not
answer correctly, repeat the questions.

Questions   *Answers*

9. What's the opposite of *simplicity*?   (Complexity.)
10. What word means "a famous person"?   (A celebrity.)
11. What's the opposite of *ordinary*?   (Special.)
12. What do we call a school of higher learning?   (A university.)
13. What's the opposite of *tragic*?   (Comical.)
14. What do you call organization from A to Z?   (Alphabetical.)
15. What word means "the same"?   (Identical.)
16. What's the opposite of *insecurity*?   (Security.)

Predictable Word Stress: Compound Nouns and Phrasal Verbs

PART ONE | Compound Nouns

Suitcase and mailbox are compound nouns. Compound nouns have two parts: suit + case and mail + box. There are many compound nouns in English. Sometimes we write the two parts as one word, like notebook. Sometimes we write the two parts as two words, like light switch.

FIGURE IT OUT

Most compound nouns have the same stress pattern.

 Listen to these compound nouns. Blacken the dot over the stressed syllable.

      EXAMPLE: doorbell

1. hallway
2. pancakes
3. sidewalk
4. horse race

5. birthday
6. paycheck
7. newspaper
8. typewriter

Which part of compound nouns has stress, the first part or the second part? Write a rule.

RULE FOR COMPOUND NOUNS

In compound nouns, the _____ part has stress.

PARTNER 1

1a. LISTENING DISCRIMINATION AND SPEAKING. Pair Practice for Compound Nouns. PARTNER 1. Use this page. PARTNER 2. Turn to page 40.

DIRECTIONS: First, you are the speaker. Read the groups of words to your partner. Stress is marked. Repeat any words your partner does not understand.

1. a. toothpaste	b. street car	c. wool coat	d. fruit juice
2. a. night club	b. gold watch	c. snow storm	d. keyboard
3. a. toy train	b. yard sale	c. boyfriend	d. saucepan
4. a. coffee pot	b. password	c. paper plate	d. mail truck
5. a. storybook	b. flag pole	c. road map	d. public school

Now you are the listener. Your partner will say some groups of words. Circle the letter of the *one* group that is *not* a compound noun.

EXAMPLE: a. living room (b.) plastic bag c. fireplace d. soup spoon

6. a. post office	b. eyelid	c. high school	d. ballpoint pen
7. a. orange juice	b. light rain	c. tablecloth	d. fingernail
8. a. silk shirt	b. wastebasket	c. parking lot	d. hand cream
9. a. ice skates	b. dining room	c. wire hanger	d. phone call
10. a. butterfly	b. sea level	c. colored paper	d. movie star

Now compare answers with your partner.

2. SPEAKING. Guided Conversation to Practice Compound Nouns.

DIRECTIONS: Here is a list of professions. Take turns asking and answering about work. Be sure to stress the first part of compound nouns.

EXAMPLE:
STUDENT 1: How do you like being a <u>bus driver</u>?
STUDENT 2: I'm not a <u>bus driver</u> anymore. I'm going to trade school to be a <u>car mechanic</u>.
STUDENT 1: Oh, I didn't know that. Good luck!

PROFESSIONS

art dealer	car mechanic	file clerk
bank teller	music teacher	rental agent
bus driver	dress designer	salesperson
bookkeeper	mail carrier	flight attendant
cab driver	hair stylist	stockbroker

MODEL CONVERSATION
STUDENT 1: How do you like being a _____?
STUDENT 2: I'm not a _____ anymore. I'm going to trade school to be a _____.
STUDENT 1: Oh, I didn't know that. Good luck!

3a. SPEAKING AND LISTENING. Pair Practice for Compound Nouns.
PARTNER 1. Use this page. PARTNER 2. Turn to page 41.

DIRECTIONS: Here is some information from the sports page of the newspaper. Answer your partner's questions about the latest baseball scores. Stress the first part of compound nouns.

BASEBALL SCOREBOARD

Game One	**Game Three**	**Game Five**
Rockland Redsocks 18	Ashland Whitesocks 16	Edgewood Indians 14
Parkville Panthers 15	Peachgrove Pitchforks 18	Deerfield Songbirds 19
Game Two	**Game Four**	
Springfield Statesmen 13	Brookport Batboys 17	
Yorktown Jetplanes 17	Homewood Greyhounds 15	

Now ask your partner about the latest basketball scores. Write the teams and scores on the scoreboard below. The first one is an example.

QUESTIONS
Who played in Game One?
Who won?
What was the score?
(Ask similar questions about the other four games.)

BASKETBALL SCOREBOARD

Game One

Waycross _Wildcats_ _30_   Kingman _____ _____

Game Four

Sunland _____ _____   Pineland _____ _____

Game Two

Glenwood _____ _____   Bayland _____ _____

Game Five

Bridgeport _____ _____   Claytown _____ _____

Game Three

Tombstone _____ _____

Lakeside _____ _____

Now compare answers with your partner.

| Two-Word Proper Nouns

United States, *Mexico City*, and *Park Avenue* are **proper nouns** with two words. We spell them with capital letters. Many proper nouns are geographical names, like countries, states, continents, cities, islands, oceans, and parks.

FIGURE IT OUT

Most two-word proper nouns have the same stress pattern. Listen to these proper nouns. Blacken the dot over the stressed syllable.

EXAMPLE: Lincoln Park

1. New York
2. South America
3. Great Britain
4. Cook Islands
5. Red Sea
6. St. Paul
7. First Avenue
8. Lake Huron

Which part of two-word proper nouns have stress, the first part or the second part? Write a rule.

RULE FOR TWO-WORD PROPER NOUNS

In two-word proper nouns, the _____ part has stress.

Exception: Listen to these examples of two-word proper nouns with the word *Street*.

Pine Street   Fifth Street   Green Street   Madison Street

Which part of these two-word proper nouns has stress?

PRACTICE ACTIVITIES

1. SPEAKING. Pair or Group Practice for Two-Word Proper Nouns.

DIRECTIONS: This is a map of the United States with some cities. Take turns asking and answering questions about the cities. Stress two-word proper nouns correctly.

EXAMPLE:

STUDENT 1:   Where's Great Falls?
STUDENT 2:   It's in Montana. Where's San Francisco?
STUDENT 3:   It's in California. Where's . . . ?

2a. LISTENING DISCRIMINATION AND SPEAKING. Pair Practice for Two-Word Proper Nouns.   PARTNER 1. Use this page. PARTNER 2. Turn to page 42.

DIRECTIONS: Does your partner know some amazing facts about the United States? Ask your partner these questions. If your partner answers wrong or does not know the answer, say the answer.

> **EXAMPLE:**
>
> YOU: What's the smallest state in the United States?
> YOUR PARTNER: Rhode Island.
> YOU: That's right.

1. What city in the United States has the most people? (New York)
2. What's the highest place in the United States? (Mount McKinley in Alaska)
3. What's the world's largest canyon? (the Grand Canyon in Arizona)
4. Which of the U.S. states is at the center of North America? (North Dakota)
5. In which U.S. state was the world's first atomic bomb set off? (New Mexico)
6. What's the world's longest natural bridge? (Landscape Arch in Utah)

Now your partner will ask you some amazing facts about the United States. Choose an answer from the word bank. Stress two-word proper nouns correctly. If you do not know the answer, your partner will tell you.

> **EXAMPLE:**
>
> YOUR PARTNER: What's the smallest state in the United States?
> YOU: Rhode Island.
> YOUR PARTNER: That's right.

WORD BANK

Battle Creek, Michigan   Kitty Hawk, North Carolina
Death Valley in California   the Mississippi River
Hawaii   New York

3. READ AND REPORT. Class Activity to Practice Two-Word Proper Nouns.

DIRECTIONS: Choose one of the topics. You can use a map, an encyclopedia or an atlas to find information. Then tell the class your answers.

1. Name four two-word cities in Texas.
2. Name the five Great Lakes in North America.
3. Name four oceans.
4. Name three parks in your city.
5. Name the ten two-word states in the United States.
6. Name ten two-word cities in California.
7. Name three famous sites in Arizona.
8. Name three two-word provinces in Canada.

Get up, *turn off*, and *run out of* are phrasal verbs. Phrasal verbs have two or three parts: *get + up*, *turn + off*, and *run + out + of*. There are many phrasal verbs in English.

 FIGURE IT OUT

Phrasal verbs have the same stress pattern. Listen to these phrasal verbs. Blacken the dot over the stressed syllable.

EXAMPLE: keep up

1. look out
2. come back
3. pick up
4. keep on

5. figure out
6. get through
7. look up to
8. put up with

Which part of phrasal verbs have stress, the first part, the second part, or the third part? Write a rule.

RULE FOR PHRASAL VERBS

In phrasal verbs, the _____ part has stress.

PRACTICE ACTIVITIES

1. SPEAKING. Guided Conversations to Practice Phrasal Verbs.

DIRECTIONS: Take turns practicing the conversations, using the given phrasal verbs and phrases. Stress the second part of phrasal verbs.

 I. EXAMPLE:

STUDENT 1: I'm having a party tonight. Can you come?
STUDENT 2: Can I come over after eight?
STUDENT 1: Oh, sure. See you then!

PHRASAL VERBS

come over   come by   drop by   drop in   show up   stop by   stop in   stop over

II. EXAMPLE:

STUDENT 1: What are you going to do this afternoon?
STUDENT 2: I plan to go over my lab work.
STUDENT 1: Do you need me to help out?
STUDENT 2: I don't think so. I can get by.

PHRASES

fill out an application
look into financial aid
look up some answers for math
go over my lab work

pick out some gifts
take back my stereo
turn in all my books
try out some new computers

2a. SPEAKING AND LISTENING. Pair Practice for Phrasal Verbs.
PARTNER 1. Use this page. PARTNER 2. Turn to page 43.

Bob is very busy. Here is Bob's agenda. It shows some things he will do in April. Your partner has Bob's April agenda, too.

DIRECTIONS: For each day with *, Bob will be busy. Ask questions about the days with *. Take turns asking and answering questions. Stress phrasal verbs correctly.

EXAMPLE:

YOU:	What will Bob do April 8th?
YOUR PARTNER:	He'll pay back a loan. What will Bob do April 16th?
YOU:	He'll get away to the mountains. What will . . .

APRIL   Bob's Agenda

SUNDAY	MONDAY	TUESDAY	WEDNESDAY	THURSDAY	FRIDAY	SATURDAY
				1	**2** try out a new tennis racket	**3** *
4 drop in on friends	**5** *	**6**	**7** work out at the gym	**8** *	**9**	**10** figure out taxes
11 *	**12** add up expenses	**13**	**14** *	**15**	**16** get away to the mountains	**17**
18 *	**19** look into night school	**20** *	**21**	**22**	**23** go out with Diane	**24** *
25 stop by the library	**26** *	**27** *	**28**	**29**	**30** pick Diane up at the airport	

3a. ROLE-PLAY. Pair Practice for Compound Nouns and Phrasal Verbs.
PARTNER 1. Use this page. PARTNER 2. Turn to page 44.

DIRECTIONS: Imagine you are an airplane passenger. Read this information:

You are in an airport in New York. You left Los Angeles at 9 A.M., stopped over in St. Louis, changed planes, and then arrived in New York at 6 P.M., two hours ago.

You realized that one of your two suitcases was lost on the flight between St. Louis and New York. You're upset about it because some toilet articles and clothes for your trip are in the lost suitcase. You got angry and you threw away your baggage claim ticket for the missing suitcase in a nearby trash can. You took your remaining suitcase and checked in at the Grand Hotel on Fifth Avenue in New York. After opening your bag, you believe the missing items in the lost suitcase are:

> a hairbrush, a toothbrush, toothpaste, underclothes, a bathrobe, two pairs of blue jeans, a sweatshirt, a raincoat, sunglasses, two newspapers, a small notebook

You are now back at the airport to try to find your lost suitcase. Your partner is the claim agent. Use the information above to answer your partner's questions. Stress compound nouns and phrasal verbs correctly.

1b. LISTENING DISCRIMINATION AND SPEAKING. Pair Practice for Compound Nouns. PARTNER 2. Use this page. PARTNER 1. Turn to page 34.

DIRECTIONS: First, you are the listener. Your partner will say some groups of words. Circle the letter of the *one* group that is *not* a compound noun.

EXAMPLE: a. living room (b.) plastic bag c. fireplace d. soup spoon

1. a. toothpaste   b. street car   c. wool coat   d. fruit juice
2. a. night club   b. gold watch   c. snow storm   d. keyboard
3. a. toy train   b. yard sale   c. boyfriend   d. saucepan
4. a. coffee pot   b. password   c. paper plate   d. mail truck
5. a. storybook   b. flag pole   c. road map   d. public school

Now you are the speaker. Read the groups of words to your partner. Word stress is marked. Repeat any words your partner does not understand.

6. a. post office   b. eyelid   c. high school   d. ballpoint pen
7. a. orange juice   b. light rain   c. tablecloth   d. fingernail
8. a. silk shirt   b. wastebasket   c. parking lot   d. hand cream
9. a. ice skates   b. dining room   c. wire hanger   d. phone call
10. a. butterfly   b. sea level   c. colored paper   d. movie star

Now compare answers with your partner.

PAIR PRACTICE: Partner 2

PARTNER 2

3b. SPEAKING AND LISTENING. Pair Practice for Compound Nouns.
Partner 2. Use this page. Partner 1. Turn to page 35.

DIRECTIONS: Here is some information from the sports page of the newspaper. Ask your partner some questions about the latest baseball scores. Write the teams and scores on the scoreboard below. The first one is an example.

QUESTIONS
Who played in Game One?
Who won?
What was the score?
(Ask similar questions about the other four games.)

BASEBALL SCOREBOARD

Game One

Rockland Redsocks 18

Parkville ______ ____

Game Two

Springfield ______ ____

Yorktown ______ ____

Game Three

Ashland ______ ____

Peachgrove ______ ____

Game Four

Brookport ______ ____

Homewood ______ ____

Game Five

Edgewood ______ ____

Deerfield ______ ____

Now answer your partner's questions about the latest basketball scores. Stress the first part of compound nouns.

BASKETBALL SCOREBOARD

Game One
Waycross Wildcats 30
Sunland Slamdunks 20

Game Two
Glenwood Hounddogs 30
Bridgeport Buckhorns 60

Game Three
Tombstone Tomcats 40
Lakeside Hardhats 70

Game Four
Kingman Tomboys 50
Pineland Pitbulls 80

Game Five
Bayland Bulldogs 60
Claytown Cowboys 40

Now compare answers with your partner.

2b. LISTENING DISCRIMINATION AND SPEAKING. Pair Practice for Two-Word Proper Nouns. PARTNER 2. Use this page. PARTNER 1. Turn to page 37.

DIRECTIONS: Your partner will ask you some amazing facts about the United States. Choose an answer from the word bank. Stress two-word proper nouns correctly. If you do not know the answer, your partner will tell you.

EXAMPLE:

YOUR PARTNER:	What's the smallest state in the United States?
YOU:	Rhode Island.
YOUR PARTNER:	That's right.

WORD BANK

the Grand Canyon in Arizona   New Mexico
Landscape Arch in Utah   New York
Mount McKinley in Alaska   North Dakota

Now does your partner know some amazing facts about the United States? Ask your partner these questions. If your partner answers wrong or does not know the answer, say the answer.

EXAMPLE:

YOU:	What's the smallest state in the United States?
YOUR PARTNER:	Rhode Island.
YOU:	That's right.

1. What's the longest river in the United States? (the Mississippi River)

2. Which U.S. state is not in North America? (Hawaii)

3. What city was the first capital of the United States? (New York)

4. Where was the world's first successful airplane flight? (Kitty Hawk, North Carolina)

5. What's the lowest place in the United States? (Death Valley in California)

6. What city makes the most breakfast cereal in the world? (Battle Creek, Michigan)

PAIR PRACTICE: Partner 2

2b. SPEAKING AND LISTENING. Pair Practice for Phrasal Verbs.

PARTNER 2. Use this page. PARTNER 1. Turn to page 39.

Bob is very busy. Here is Bob's agenda. It shows some things he will do in April. Your partner has Bob's April agenda, too.

DIRECTIONS: For each day with *, Bob will be busy. Ask questions about the days with *. Take turns asking and answering questions. Stress phrasal verbs correctly.

EXAMPLE:

YOU: What will Bob do April 16th?
YOUR PARTNER: He'll get away to the mountains. What will Bob do April 8th?
YOU: He'll pay back a loan. What will . . .

APRIL — Bob's Agenda

SUNDAY	MONDAY	TUESDAY	WEDNESDAY	THURSDAY	FRIDAY	SATURDAY
				1	**2** *	**3** find out about flights to Miami
4 *	**5** drop off clothes at the cleaners	**6**	**7** *	**8** pay back a loan	**9**	**10** *
11 call up parents	**12** *	**13**	**14** make up a test	**15**	**16** *	**17**
18 come back from the mountains	**19** *	**20** pick up some groceries	**21**	**22**	**23** *	**24** pick out a stereo
25 *	**26** drop off Diane at the airport	**27** turn in an essay	**28**	**29**	**30** *	

3b. ROLE-PLAY. Pair Practice for Compound Nouns and Phrasal Verbs.
PARTNER 2. Use this page. PARTNER 1. Turn to page 40.

DIRECTIONS: Imagine you are an airport employee. Read this information:

You are in an airport in New York. You are the claim agent, and your job is to make reports on lost baggage. Your partner is a passenger who lost something in flight. The passenger has come to you to file a claim. Ask your partner the following questions. Stress compound nouns and phrasal verbs correctly.

(First open your conversation with the passenger.)

Hello. I'm the claim agent for the New York airport. I'd like to ask you a few questions.

1. What city were you flying from?
2. What time did your flight take off?
3. Did you stop over?
4. When did your flight to New York get in?
5. What kind of baggage did you lose?
6. Did you lose it after you stopped over?
7. Please describe the contents of your lost suitcase so that I can fill out a checklist.
8. Did you lose any identification papers, such as a passport?
9. Did you lose any money or a billfold, coin purse, checkbook, credit cards, or traveler's checks?
10. May I see your claim ticket from the missing suitcase?
11. What hotel did you check into?

(Now close your conversation with the passenger.)

Please don't worry about it. We're sure your suitcase will turn up. I'll look into it personally. A claim agent will call you when your bag turns up. We're sorry. We hope you can get by without it for a day or two. Enjoy your stay in New York.

PAIR PRACTICE: Partner 2

Sentence Stress

PART ONE	Stressed Words in Sentences

You have already learned about stressed syllables in words. Now you will learn that some words and syllables in sentences are stressed, too. Stressed words and syllables in sentences are long and loud. Some of them are high, too.

 Here are some example sentences with stress marked. Study them.

1. He works in a factory.
2. The doctor called a patient.
3. The schedule changes in spring.
4. She remembered to bring a calculator.
5. Visitors come by car and by bus.
6. They left their tickets at home.

FIGURE IT OUT

Which words are stressed in these example sentences? Write some rules.

RULES FOR STRESSED WORDS

1. Nouns and verbs are *(circle one)*   stressed   unstressed.
2. Prepositions, articles, and pronouns are *(circle one)*   stressed   unstressed.

Now here are some more example sentences with stress marked. Study them.

1. That patient has a bad headache.
2. This restaurant is very expensive.
3. His new car was small, fast, and expensive.
4. Some students will read that long story.
5. They can take short messages for you.
6. The manager is holding a brief meeting.

FIGURE IT OUT

Which new groups of words are stressed in these example sentences? Write some rules.

RULES FOR SENTENCE STRESS

1. Adjectives are *(circle one)*   stressed   unstressed.
2. *This, that, these,* and *those* are *(circle one)*   stressed   unstressed.
3. *To be, to have,* and helping verbs are *(circle one)*   stressed   unstressed.

Now here is one more group of example sentences with stress marked. Study them.

1. I'm not talking and joking loudly.
2. Junie wasn't able to type quickly.
3. They don't often call after midnight.
4. Where does he live and what does he do?
5. Why did they come late but leave early?
6. Who will call and make an appointment?

FIGURE IT OUT

Which new groups of words are stressed in these example sentences? Write some rules.

RULES FOR SENTENCE STRESS

1. Adverbs are *(circle one)*   stressed   unstressed.
2. Negative words are *(circle one)*   stressed   unstressed.
3. *Wh-* question words are *(circle one)*   stressed   unstressed.
4. Conjunctions *(and, but, if)* are *(circle one)*   stressed   unstressed.

PRACTICE ACTIVITIES

1. READ ALOUD.

DIRECTIONS: Read the groups of example sentences aloud on pages 45 and 46. Say the stressed words long and loud. Say the unstressed words short and quiet.

2. READ ALOUD.

DIRECTIONS: First, complete each sentence with your own words. Next, use your RULES FOR SENTENCE STRESS to put a dot over the *stressed* words in your sentences. Then, read your sentences aloud to a partner or to the class.

EXAMPLE:

They to don't want. . .
They don't want to **do their homework.**

1. They sometimes go . . .

2. It's not easy to . . .

3. When will you . . .

4. After a long test . . .

5. A strange man . . .

6. He doesn't really have time to . . .

7. How many times did . . .

8. I cook well, but . . .

9. The instructor can't . . .

10. We'd like to know more about . . .

11. This notebook isn't . . .

12. On a sunny day in February . . .

PART TWO Regular Rhythm and Rhythm Groups

In sentences, you hear stressed syllables and words with unstressed syllables and words between them. Stress and unstress usually alternate to make a pattern. This regular pattern is called **rhythm**.

It's time for the movie to start.

Our team has won the game again.

The tools for the job are easy to find.

The last person to leave can lock the door.

Be sure to call me as soon as possible.

Now listen to and repeat the sentences. Tap a finger or pencil for each stressed syllable or word.

Like unstressed syllables in words, most unstressed syllables and words in sentences have the vowel sound /ə/ or /ɪ/.

Listen to the syllables and words without stress in these sentences; they sound like /ə/ or /ɪ/.

The name at the top of the list was Adam's.

They had lots of time but little money.

A storm will hit later tonight.

I can give them an answer in an hour.

She bought him a ticket before the concert began.

Now listen to and repeat the sentences. Say the stressed syllables high, long, and loud. Say the unstressed syllables low, short, and quiet. Pronounce unstressed vowels like /ə/ or /ɪ/.

In longer sentences, speakers say words in **rhythm groups**. There are very short pauses between rhythm groups.

Listen to these longer sentences marked in rhythm groups:

I need some more time / to finish the exercise.

She's catching a flight / at eight in the morning.

The computer in the office / has been down for an hour.

His lecture on earthquakes / was easy to understand.

Students in the Drama Club / will be performing this weekend.

How many stressed syllables do you find in each rhythm group?

How many unstressed syllables do you find in each rhythm group?

Are there any rhythm groups with *no* stressed syllables?

Now listen to and repeat the sentences. Say the words in rhythm groups. Pronounce the stressed syllables high, long, and loud. Pronounce the unstressed syllables low, short, and quiet.

PRACTICE ACTIVITIES

1. READ ALOUD.

DIRECTIONS: Here are some long sentences. Practice reading them in rhythm groups.

1. The rent is due / the first of the month.
2. You'll find a mailbox / a block down the street.
3. Please leave your number / and I'll call you later.
4. The date of the test / was announced in class.
5. The store will be open / from nine to nine.
6. We were best friends / during high school and college.
7. How did the study give proof / that the most visible cars / are white and red?
8. They made reservations / to take a vacation / the last week of June.
9. I'm reading an article / about the latest research / on improving memory.
10. When I came in the room, / Ken was on the phone / taking a message.

2. LISTENING DISCRIMINATION.

DIRECTIONS: You are going to hear some long sentences. Put a line (/) between the rhythm groups you hear.

EXAMPLE:

Seven new students / have joined our class.

1. She likes to spend weekends playing golf and tennis.
2. Ann's been studying piano for more than a year.
3. The cause of the accident is completely unknown.
4. Crime has increased in urban areas across the nation.
5. The movie director used indirect lighting for a special effect.
6. Brad didn't need help finding the tools to repair the plumbing.
7. The instructor hasn't told us how many papers are required for the course.
8. How many times do I need to tell you not to call after midnight?

Now read these sentences aloud. Practice reading them in rhythm groups.

3a. LISTENING DISCRIMINATION AND SPEAKING. Pair Practice Picture for Rhythm Groups. PARTNER 1. Use this page. PARTNER 2. Turn to page 53.

DIRECTIONS: You are traveling and you meet your partner at a gas station. You need some directions. Here is a list of the towns you are trying to find. Use sentence stress and rhythm groups in your questions.

EXAMPLE:

YOU:	How can I get to / a town called Fairwood?
YOUR PARTNER:	Fairwood's on Highway 7 / between Troy and Bishop.
YOU:	Thanks. And how can I get to / a town called Granite?

TOWNS TO FIND

Boone Clinton Dodge Edison Fairwood Granite Newport Richmond

Now you're at a gas station and your partner wants directions. Use the map below to answer your partner's questions. Use sentence stress and rhythm groups in your answers.

EXAMPLE:

YOUR PARTNER:	How can I get to / a town called Oakland?
YOU:	Oakland's on Interstate 2 / between Kingston and Vista.
YOUR PARTNER:	Thanks. And how can I get to . . .

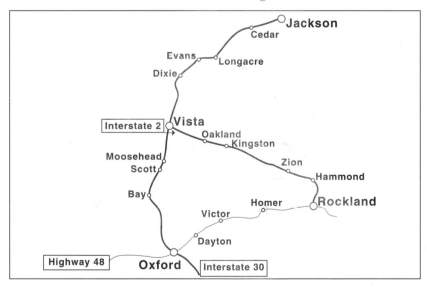

4. READ AND REPORT. News Show. Small Group or Class Practice for Sentence Stress and Rhythm Groups.

DIRECTIONS: Choose one of the roles below.

ROLES: International News, National News, Local News, Business News, Feature Story, Health and Fitness News, Fashion, Entertainment, Sports, Weather, Commercials.

Your instructor will give you today's newspaper. Use a newspaper story to prepare a two- to four-minute news report. If your role is *commercials*, use two different advertisements to prepare two 30-second commercials. Use sentence stress and rhythm groups in your report. Your instructor can record your show on cassette for the class to hear "radio" news. For "TV" news, your instructor may videotape.

Focus means that one word or syllable in a sentence is higher, longer, and louder than all others.

Look at and listen to these regular sentences and compare them with focus sentences.

Regular Sentences	Focus Sentences
Please put your books away.	Please put your books away.
He wants to rent a car.	He wants to rent a car.
Joanne is the youngest daughter.	Joanne is the youngest daughter.
Your glasses are in the car.	Your glasses are in the car.

Focus is a kind of sentence stress for speech longer than one sentence, like in conversations and reports. Prepositions, articles, and pronouns are not usually stressed, but a speaker can use focus on any word in a sentence to:

1. *Correct something that has already been said*

LYNN: She wore a lovely white dress. (regular sentence)

MAY: Well, not really. She wore a pink dress. (focus sentence)

MR. SANDS: Two hundred workers were laid off. (regular sentence)

MR. BURNS: I believe three hundred were laid off. (focus sentence)

2. *Introduce new information in conversation*

TIMMY: I'm going to ask for a tennis racket. (regular sentence)

TOMMY: You need a beginner's tennis racket. (*beginner's* = new information)

CAROL: Today we went to the lab. (regular sentence)

DAVID: You'd better watch out for the chemicals in the lab. (*chemicals* = new information)

3. *Create special attention or emphasis on one word*

JOE: Why didn't you say something?

SAM: Because I didn't think it was polite to interrupt.

CALVIN: She doesn't type very fast.

MELVIN: Of course not. This is the first time she's tried!

4. *Contrast two words*

Bobby wants chocolate, and Beverly wants vanilla.

The milk is in the refrigerator. The fruit is next to it.

Video tapes are on the second floor. Books are on the first.

1. LISTENING DISCRIMINATION.

DIRECTIONS: Listen to the pairs of sentences. *One* of the sentences uses focus for emphasis. Circle the letter of the sentence with focus.

EXAMPLE:

a. This man doesn't know what to do.

ⓑ This man doesn't know what to do.

1. a. Put your books in your desk.
   b. Put your books in your desk.
2. a. I don't like this music.
   b. I don't like this music.
3. a. I mailed the letter yesterday.
   b. I mailed the letter yesterday.
4. a. You're supposed to sit in a window seat.
   b. You're supposed to sit in a window seat.
5. a. Do you want to give money for a gift?
   b. Do you want to give money for a gift?

6. a. Add two cups of sugar.
   b. Add two cups of sugar.
7. a. What do you think of it?
   b. What do you think of it?
8. a. He was the first person to ask.
   b. He was the first person to ask.
9. a. The remote is near the TV.
   b. The remote is near the TV.
10. a. She told us not to go there.
    b. She told us not to go there.

2. SPEAKING. Guided Conversations to Practice Sentence Stress and Focus.
DIRECTIONS: Study the example conversations. Use the examples and lists to create conversations with a partner. Stress your sentences correctly and use focus for new information and emphasis.

 I. EXAMPLE:

STUDENT 1: I hear you're doing well in statistics.

STUDENT 2: Actually, I took statistics last year. Now I'm taking psychology.

STUDENT 1: Oh, psychology's easy. I bet you love it.

STUDENT 2: Well, no, you love it. I'm barely passing!

LIST OF CLASSES

| anatomy | chemistry | design | geology | mechanics | physics | statistics |
| business | Chinese` | economics | health | psychology | sociology | theater |

 II. EXAMPLE:

STUDENT 1: I bought some pairs of shoes today.

STUDENT 2: How many pairs of shoes?

STUDENT 1: Five. That's not very many.

STUDENT 2: Are you kidding? I don't buy five pairs of shoes in a year!

LIST OF PURCHASES

belts	pairs of shoes	pairs of gym socks
compact disks	highlighter pens	combs
shirts	typewriter ribbons	
videotapes	pairs of shorts	

3a. SPEAKING AND LISTENING. What Would You Like? Pair Practice for Sentence Stress and Focus. PARTNER 1. Use this page. PARTNER 2. Turn to page 54.

DIRECTIONS: You are shopping, and your partner is a salesperson. Use the phrases to say what you would like. Listen to the salesperson's response and then correct the salesperson with focus. Study the example.

EXAMPLE: (cue). . . black wool hat.

SALESPERSON: What would you like?

SHOPPER: I'd like a black wool hat.

SALESPERSON: Here you are. This is our best black cotton hat.

SHOPPER: I'm sorry, but maybe you misunderstood. I said a black wool hat.

1. . . . a pocket dictionary.
2. . . . a canvas bookbag.
3. . . . a brown leather belt.
4. . . . a seat by the window.
5. . . . a ticket for the one o'clock show.
6. . . . a tent for camping.

Now you are the salesperson and your partner is shopping. Listen to the shopper and then use the phrases to offer an item. The shopper needs to correct you with focus. Study the example.

EXAMPLE: (cue) . . . Rolex watch

SALESPERSON: What would you like?

SHOPPER: I'd like a Timex watch.

SALESPERSON: Here you are. This is our best Rolex watch.

SHOPPER: I'm sorry, but maybe you misunderstood. I said a Timex watch.

7. . . . red bowtie.
8. . . . easy chair.
9. . . . pair of headsets.
10. . . . table behind the bandstand.
11. . . . 90-minute tape.
12. . . . laptop computer.

4a. ROLE-PLAY. Pair Practice for Sentence Stress and Focus.
PARTNER 1. Use this page. PARTNER 2. Turn to page 54.

DIRECTIONS: Imagine you have just returned from a vacation. Read this information:

You spent two weeks in Italy. You took a jet to Rome and stayed with two friends there. You rented a car and toured some famous cities. You visited churches in Florence, and you rode a boat in the canals of Venice. Then you went back to Rome and visited some museums. You loved Italy, but you didn't care for the food at all. What's more, everyone served you wine, and you don't drink wine. Generally, though, you enjoyed your vacation and you believe Italy is a charming place.

You are now back home, and one of your classmates is going to ask you some questions and make some comments about your trip. Use the information above to correct your classmate's questions and comments. Use focus in your responses.

3b. LISTENING DISCRIMINATION AND SPEAKING. Pair Practice Picture for Rhythm Groups. PARTNER 2. Use this page. PARTNER 1. Turn to page 49.

DIRECTIONS: You're at a gas station and your partner wants directions. Use the map below to answer your partner's questions. Use sentence stress and rhythm groups in your answers.

EXAMPLE:

YOUR PARTNER: How can I get to / a town called Fairwood?

YOU: Fairwood's on Highway 7 / between Troy and Bishop.

YOUR PARTNER: Thanks. And how can I get to . . .

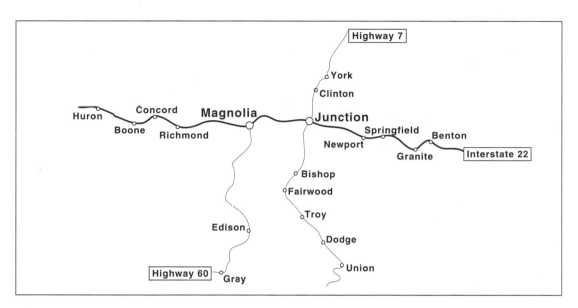

Now you are traveling and you meet your partner at a gas station. You need some directions. Here is a list of the towns you are trying to find. Use sentence stress and rhythm groups in your questions.

EXAMPLE:

YOU: How can I get to / a town called Oakland?

YOUR PARTNER: Oakland's on Interstate 2 / between Kingston and Vista.

YOU: Thanks. And how can I get to / a town called Evans?

TOWNS TO FIND

Bay	Homer
Cedar	Moosehead
Dayton	Oakland
Evans	Zion

3b. SPEAKING AND LISTENING. What Would You Like? Pair Practice for Sentence Stress and Focus.   PARTNER 2. Use this page. PARTNER 1. Turn to page 52.

DIRECTIONS: You are a salesperson and your partner is shopping. Listen to the shopper and then use the phrases to offer an item. The shopper needs to correct you with focus. Study the example.

EXAMPLE: (cue) . . . black cotton hat.

SALESPERSON: What would you like?

SHOPPER: I'd like a black wool hat.

SALESPERSON: Here you are. This is our best black cotton hat.

SHOPPER: I'm sorry, but maybe you misunderstood. I said a black wool hat.

1. . . . desk dictionary.
2. . . . canvas sports bag.
3. . . . black leather belt.

4. . . . seat by the aisle.
5. . . . ticket for the three o'clock show.
6. . . . stove for camping.

Now you are shopping, and your partner is the salesperson. Use the phrases to say what you would like. Listen to the salesperson's response and then correct the salesperson with focus. Study the example.

EXAMPLE: (cue) . . . Timex watch.

SALESPERSON: What would you like?

SHOPPER: I'd like a Timex watch.

SALESPERSON: Here you are. This is our best Rolex watch.

SHOPPER: I'm sorry, but maybe you misunderstood. I said a Timex watch.

7. . . . a red necktie.
8. . . . a rocking chair.
9. . . . a pair of speakers.

10. . . . a table near the bandstand.
11. . . . a 60-minute tape.
12. . . . a desktop computer.

4b. ROLE-PLAY. Pair Practice for Sentence Stress and Focus.
PARTNER 2. Use this page. PARTNER 1. Turn to page 52.

DIRECTIONS: Imagine your partner has just come back from a vacation. Ask your partner these questions and make these comments about the vacation. Your partner will respond with focus.

1. So, how was your trip to Spain?
2. Did it take a long time to go by boat?
3. I hear you stayed with your family. How are they?
4. Did you like riding the train in Italy?
5. I've heard the canals in Florence are great!
6. What did you think of the churches in Rome?
7. I'm sure the food is wonderful there.
8. Didn't you just love the wine?
9. Wow! It sounds like your vacation was terrible.
10. Italy is such an awful place! Don't you agree?

PAIR PRACTICE: Partner 2

Sentence Stress, Linking, and Blending

In Lesson 6, you learned about sentence stress and rhythm. Now you are going to learn about sounds in rhythm groups.

PART ONE Linking Consonant to Vowel

 Here are some words and pairs of words. Listen to them. Compare them.

minute, wi<u>n i</u>t	letter, le<u>t h</u>er
tower, ho<u>w a</u>re	often, o<u>ff a</u>n
pocket, loc<u>k i</u>t	liver, li<u>ve o</u>r
goddess, go<u>t u</u>s	career, you<u>r e</u>ar
planet, pla<u>n i</u>t	deny, a<u>n e</u>ye
terror, whe<u>re a</u>re	frozen, know<u>s a</u>n

The words and pairs of words sound alike.

FIGURE IT OUT
Study the pairs of words above. What is the last sound in the first word?
(*circle one*)   consonant   vowel

What is the first sound in the second word? (*circle one*)   consonant   vowel
Now write a rule.

RULE FOR LINKING CONSONANT TO VOWEL

When the last sound of a word in a rhythm group is a _____ and the first

sound in the following word is a _____, pronounce them like one word.

This joining of two or more words in a rhythm group is called **linking**.

Disappearing /h/

In spoken English, unstressed pronouns beginning with /h/, like *he, her,* and *him,* usually drop the /h/ sound after a consonant.

[▭] Listen to these sentences:

> Gi<u>ve (h)</u>er a dollar.
> I<u>s (h)</u>e ready to go?
> I tol<u>d (h)</u>im to call me.

Words ending in consonants are linked before *he, her,* and *him.* Without /h/, these unstressed pronouns begin with a vowel.

[▭] **INTENSIVE PRACTICE**

As a class, listen to and repeat the words and pairs of words you hear.

> **EXAMPLE:**
>
> shout, ru<u>sh out</u>

PRACTICE ACTIVITIES

1. READ ALOUD.

DIRECTIONS: Practice linking consonants to vowels in rhythm groups.

/p/

Sto<u>p o</u>ver at 8 / and dro<u>p o</u>ff my books.
Go to slee<u>p e</u>arly / and wake u<u>p a</u>t 7.

/t/

She's no<u>t at a</u>ll tired, / bu<u>t it</u>'s still early.
We go<u>t out o</u>f the meeting / a<u>t e</u>leven thirty.

/d/

I ha<u>d a</u> good time / on my weeken<u>d o</u>ff.
Instea<u>d o</u>f studying, / we ro<u>de aroun</u>d i<u>n</u> the car.

/k/

After a wee<u>k o</u>f tests, / we too<u>k o</u>ff for Hawaii.
When you ba<u>ck up</u>, / loo<u>k ou</u>t for other cars.

/s/

The trip take<u>s an</u> hour / by bu<u>s or</u> car.
The pla<u>ce is</u> familiar, / but the addres<u>s isn</u>'t.

/z/

When'<u>s (h)</u>e coming / and where'<u>s (h)</u>e staying?
He'<u>s a</u>lready noticed / that she'<u>s a</u>bsent.

/m/

The proble<u>m is</u> / so<u>me of</u> the<u>m a</u>ren't here.
I don't have ti<u>me o</u>ff, / so I can't co<u>me o</u>ver.

/n/

He works i<u>n an o</u>ffice / o<u>n E</u>ast Avenue.
I ra<u>n into</u> a friend / wh<u>en I</u> was shopping.

/r/

They're announcing the news / in March or April.
For information, / please call her on Monday.

/l/

Tomorrow we'll ask him / to tell us about it.
The final exam / was full of trick questions.

2. LISTENING DISCRIMINATION.

DIRECTIONS: You are going to hear linking in short sentences and questions. Circle the
letter of the sentence or question you hear.

EXAMPLE: I've accepted.

(a.) I've accepted.   b. I'd accepted.

1. a. She had a cold.   b. She has a cold.

2. a. You owe it.   b. You own it.

3. a. Put us up.   b. Pull us up.

4. a. Where are we meeting?   b. When are we meeting?

5. a. Did you like it?   b. Did you light it?

6. a. It's for us.   b. It's from us.

7. a. We'll trap (h)im.   b. We'll track (h)im.

8. a. She's asked you.   b. She'd asked you.

9. a. I'll laugh at it.   b. I laughed at it.

10. a. Can you shake it?   b. Can you shape it?

3. SPEAKING. Guided Conversation to Practice Linking Consonants to Vowels.

DIRECTIONS: Here is a list of topics. Take turns asking and answering about a journal
article. Be sure to link ending consonants before vowels.

EXAMPLE:
STUDENT 1:   Here's an interesting article for you.
STUDENT 2:   What's it about?
STUDENT 1:   Career options.
STUDENT 2:   Sounds awful, but thanks anyway.

JOURNAL TOPICS

college admissions   modern architecture
the Greek alphabet   the Stone Age
car insurance   checking accounts
chemical analysis   nuclear energy
the North American Free Trade Agreement   career options
new job opportunities   research institutes
world economy

4. SPEAKING. Proverbs. Practice for Linking Consonants to Vowels.

DIRECTIONS: Match the first part of each proverb in Column A with the second part in Column B. Then read the proverbs aloud in rhythm groups and use linking. Choose one of them and explain its meaning to the class.

A

1. Out of sight / d
2. Where there's a will / g
3. Don't put all your eggs / & h
4. You can lead a horse to water / j
5. Birds of a feather / a
6. Home is / i
7. When the cat's away / b
8. A place for everything / c
9. Speech is silver / e
10. Rome / f

B

a. flock together.
b. the mice will play.
c. and everything in its place.
d. out of mind.
e. and silence is golden.
f. wasn't built in a day.
g. there's a way.
h. in one basket.
i. where the heart is.
j. but you can't make it drink.

PARTNER 1

5a. LISTENING DISCRIMINATION AND SPEAKING. Pair Practice Complaints for Linking. PARTNER 1. Use this page. PARTNER 2. Turn to page 63.

PARTNER 2. Turn to page 63.

DIRECTIONS: Say the complaints below to your partner. Your partner will respond with a phrasal verb. If your partner does not make a logical response, repeat the complaint.

EXAMPLE:

YOU: I can't finish it today!
YOUR PARTNER: Put it off.

1. The light is still on!
2. This application form is blank!
3. My jacket's too warm!
4. I know I'll forget his name!
5. My new TV doesn't work!
6. I missed a test!
7. I'm supposed to wear a tie!
8. The radio's too loud!

Now your partner will complain. Respond to each complaint with a phrasal verb + *it*. You will need to use linking in your responses.

EXAMPLE:

YOUR PARTNER: This book is boring!
YOU: Put it away.

PHRASAL VERB BANK

hand in	put down	think over	take back
clean up	hang up	look up	take off

PART TWO

Linking Vowel to Vowel

 Listen to linking with words ending in /iy/, /ey/, /ay/, and /ɔy/ before a vowel sound.

/iy/ + *vowel*	/ey/ + *vowel*	/ay/ + *vowel*	/ɔy/ + *vowel*
s<u>ee u</u>s	th<u>ey a</u>lways	wh<u>y a</u>re	b<u>oy i</u>s
w<u>e o</u>ften	s<u>ay i</u>t	<u>I a</u>nswer	enj<u>oy i</u>t
k<u>ey i</u>s	w<u>ay o</u>ut	m<u>y a</u>rm	ann<u>oy u</u>s

FIGURE IT OUT

Now listen to the pairs of words again. What sound links vowel to vowel?
Write a rule.

RULE FOR LINKING /iy/, /ey/, /ay/, OR /ɔy/ TO VOWELS

When the last sound of a word in a rhythm group ends in /iy/, /ey/, /ay/, or /ɔy/ and the first sound in the following word begins with a vowel, use the sound /___/ to link.

 INTENSIVE PRACTICE

As a class, listen to and repeat the words and pairs of words you hear.

EXAMPLE:
buy, b<u>uy i</u>t

 Listen to linking with words ending in /uw/, /ow/, and /aw/.

/uw/ + *vowel*	/ow/ + *vowel*	/aw/ + *vowel*
wh<u>o i</u>s	kn<u>ow u</u>s	h<u>ow a</u>re
y<u>ou a</u>sk	g<u>o o</u>n	n<u>ow i</u>s
d<u>o a</u>ll	gr<u>ow u</u>p	h<u>ow o</u>ften

FIGURE IT OUT

Now listen to the pairs of words again. What sound links vowel to vowel?
Write a rule.

RULE FOR LINKING /uw/, /ow/, OR /aw/ TO VOWELS

When the last sound of a word in a rhythm group ends in /uw/, /ow/, or /aw/ and the first sound in the following word begins with a vowel, use the sound /___/ to link.

 INTENSIVE PRACTICE

As a class, listen to and repeat the words and pairs of words you hear.

EXAMPLE:
blue, bl<u>ue e</u>yes

1. READ ALOUD.

DIRECTIONS: Practice linking vowels to vowels in rhythm groups.

/iy/

She often jogs / in the afternoon.
Sometimes we argue / and disagree on things.
The boss really isn't able / to see anyone now.

/ey/

I can't stay awake / and pay attention.
They always leave cash / and pay at the desk.
Students may ask questions / the day of the test.

/ay/

I arranged for a meeting / in my office.
Why are you wearing / your tie and hat?
You should try it on / before you buy it.

/ɔy/

Don't annoy us / with your questions.
If the check's no good, / destroy it.
I enjoy eating fruit / after a meal.

/uw/

She's got one shoe on / and one shoe off.
Who am I going to ask / to do it?
The new equipment / is far too expensive.

/ow/

If you know (h)is address, / show up at seven.
Show us the music / and we'll follow along.
Although I guessed, / I know I was right.

/aw/

They don't allow us / to use dictionaries.
Somehow I lost it, / and now it's gone.
Now and then, / I ask how (h)e's doing.

2. SPEAKING. Guided Conversation to Practice Linking Vowels to Vowels.

DIRECTIONS: Take turns as Student 1 and Student 2. Use the example and list of adjectives to create conversations. Be sure to link ending vowels before vowels.

EXAMPLE:
STUDENT 1:   Let's go out.
STUDENT 2:   Not me. I want to stay in. I'm just too unhappy!
STUDENT 1:   Why are you unhappy?
STUDENT 2:   I don't know why I am.

ADJECTIVES

exhausted	overwhelmed	annoyed
unhappy	anxious	irritated
angry	ill	agitated

3. SPEAKING. Proverbs. Practice for Linking Vowels to Vowels.

DIRECTIONS: Match the first part of each proverb in Column A with the second part in Column B. Then read the proverbs aloud in rhythm groups and use linking. Choose one of them and explain its meaning to the class.

A

1. There are two sides /
2. Pretty is /
3. When in Rome /
4. The early bird /
5. Honesty is /
6. Strike /
7. The squeaky wheel /
8. As you make your bed /
9. The grass is always greener /
10. A bird in the hand /

B

a. so you must lie in it.
b. while the iron is hot.
c. on the other side of the fence.
d. is worth two in the bush.
e. to every story.
f. gets the oil.
g. as pretty does.
h. do as the Romans do.
i. catches the worm.
j. the best policy.

4. INTERVIEW. Pair Practice for Linking Vowels to Vowels.

DIRECTIONS: Interview a partner about going out. Use the cues to ask questions. You can take notes to help you remember your partner's answers. Your partner will interview you, too. Choose who will ask or answer first. After the interviews, use your notes to tell the class about your partner.

CUES

How often do you . . .

1. go out on dates?
2. go on double dates?
3. show up late for a date?
4. stay out after midnight?
5. stay out all night?

6. enjoy eating in restaurants?
7. see a movie?
8. see a concert or play?
9. go out of town?

PART THREE Blending Consonant to Consonant

Here are some pairs of words. The consonant sound at the end of each first word is the same as the consonant sound at the beginning of the second word.

 How many times do you hear the double consonants pronounced? Listen.

/t/	hot tea	/r/	we're ready
/p/	sharp pin	/l/	full load
/k/	black coat	/dʒ/	orange juice
/d/	bad day	/tʃ/	beach chair
/g/	big girl	/ʃ/	British ship
/m/	some money	/s/	this song
/n/	phone number	/v/	expensive vase

When two of the same consonant sounds are between words in a rhythm group, **blend** them together like one long consonant. The two consonants are *not pronounced two times*.

 Now listen to the pairs of words again and repeat them.

1. READ ALOUD.

DIRECTIONS: Practice blending consonants to consonants in rhythm groups.

1. /r/, /t/   Your dinner reservations / were made at ten.

2. /r/, /l/   I saw a car wreck / in the car pool lane.

3. /m/, /t/   She'd made the same mistake / eight times.

4. /t/, /s/   He wore a white tie / and a nice suit.

5. /t/, /g/   The best team's ready / for the big game.

6. /f/, /k/   We'll have a safe flight / from the Atlantic coast.

7. /t/, /d/   Make a left turn / after the road detour.

8. /l/, /r/   I'll listen to the weather report / on the car radio.

9. /t/, /r/   The debate team / made the honor roll.

10. /tʃ/, /r/   Each chair must be moved/ to another room.

2. SPEAKING. Guided Conversations to Practice Blending Consonants to Consonants.

DIRECTIONS: Take turns as Student 1 and Student 2. Use the examples and lists to create your conversations. Be sure to blend consonants to consonants.

I. EXAMPLE:

STUDENT 1:   I got a good deal at the appliance store today.
STUDENT 2:   Oh, really? What did you buy?
STUDENT 1:   A new electric clock.

APPLIANCES

electric kitchen knife   electric kettle
gas stove   food dehydrator
automatic can opener   rice steamer
electric clock   electric coffee maker
cassette tape player

II. EXAMPLE:

STUDENT 1:   We need some office supplies from the store room.
STUDENT 2:   What type of supplies?
STUDENT 1:   Some file labels.

SUPPLIES

stamp pads   felt-tip pens
typewriter ribbons   binder rings
book covers   file labels
desk calendars   pencil leads
plastic cups   transparent tape

3a. SPEAKING AND LISTENING ROLE-PLAY. Job Applicants. Pair Practice for Blending Consonants to Consonants. PARTNER 1. Use this page. PARTNER 2. Turn to page 64.

DIRECTIONS: Imagine you and your partner are going to interview some applicants for a job tomorrow. Each of you has information about the applicants that the other does not have. Take turns asking and answering questions about their names and present job positions.

EXAMPLE:

YOU: Who's our 10 o'clock appointment?
YOUR PARTNER: Grace Simmons. What's Mike Clark's present job?
YOU: He's an assistant typist. Who's . . .

APPLICANTS FOR JOB OPENING

Appointment	Name	Present Job
9:00	George Jones	_____
9:30	Matt Thompson	_____
10:00	*Grace Simmons*	bank clerk
10:30	Sam Moore	_____
11:00	_____	ticket taker
11:30	Susan Norton	_____
1:00	Fred Davis	_____
1:30	_____	substitute teacher
2:00	Mike Clark	assistant typist
2:30	Janet Taylor	_____
3:00	Phil Landon	_____
3:30	Meg Gibson	window washer

5b. LISTENING DISCRIMINATION AND SPEAKING. Pair Practice Complaints for Linking. PARTNER 2. Use this page. PARTNER 1. Turn to page 58.

DIRECTIONS: Your partner will complain. Respond to each complaint with a phrasal verb + *it*. You will need to use linking in your responses.

EXAMPLE:

YOUR PARTNER: I can't fini<u>sh it</u> today!
YOU: Pu<u>t it o</u>ff.

PHRASAL VERB BANK

take off   make up   write down   fill out   turn off   put on   turn down   take back

Now say the complaints below to your partner. Your partner will respond with a phrasal verb. If your partner does not make a logical response, repeat the complaint.

EXAMPLE:

YOU: This boo<u>k is</u> boring!
YOUR PARTNER: Pu<u>t it</u> away.

1. My coat's on the floor!
2. This book is overdue!
3. This suitcase is heavy!
4. My English essay is two days late!
5. My belt is too tight!
6. I don't know how to spell a word!
7. I spilled my coffee!
8. I don't like making quick decisions!

3b. SPEAKING AND LISTENING ROLE-PLAY. Job Applicants. Pair Practice for Blending Consonants to Consonants. PARTNER 2. Use this page. PARTNER 1. Turn to page 63.

DIRECTIONS: Imagine you and your partner are going to interview some applicants for a job tomorrow. Each of you has information about the applicants that the other does not have. Take turns asking and answering questions about their names and present job positions.

EXAMPLE:

YOU:	Who's our 1 o'clock appointment?
YOUR PARTNER:	Fred Davis. What's Susan Norton's present job?
YOU:	She's a music composer. Who's...

APPLICANTS FOR JOB OPENING

Appointment	Name	Present Job
9:00	_____	newspaper reporter
9:30	Matt Thompson	car rental agent
10:00	Grace Simmons	_____
10:30	_____	academic counselor
11:00	Patrick Cain	_____
11:30	Susan Norton	music composer
1:00	*Fred Davis*	film maker
1:30	Isabel Lewis	_____
2:00	Mike Clark	_____
2:30	_____	insurance salesperson
3:00	_____	computer repairman
3:30	Meg Gibson	_____

Rising/Falling Intonation

There are generally three tones in an English sentence or question. They are like musical notes.

high	_____
medium	_____
low	_____

Here is an English sentence. Listen to the tones.

EXAMPLE:

high		Mon	
medium		Today's	
low			day.

The sentence starts on the medium tone, rises to the high tone, and then falls to the low tone. This is *rising/falling* intonation. *Rising/falling* intonation is shown with an arrow like this:

Today's Monday. I'm going to go to work.

Here is an English *yes/no* question. Listen to the tones.

EXAMPLE:

high		leaving?
medium	Are they	
low		

The question starts on the medium tone and rises to the high tone. This is *rising* intonation. *Rising* intonation is shown with an arrow like this:

Are they leaving? Did it take a long time?

These are the two basic English intonation patterns. This lesson is about stressed words and *rising/falling* intonation.

PART ONE

Statements and Commands

Statements and commands can be negative or affirmative. Listen to these examples:

> The library opens at seven. (affirmative statement)
> We didn't buy any tickets. (negative statement)
> Turn left on Fourth Street. (affirmative command)
> Don't leave your coat on the chair. (negative command)

LISTENING DISCRIMINATION.

DIRECTIONS: Listen to these statements and commands. Circle the letter of the intonation you hear.

EXAMPLE:

They've just spoken. (a.) b.

1. I need to do my homework. a. b.
2. She's never been to Texas. a. b.
3. You don't have to answer. a. b.
4. Call me a little later. a. b.
5. Send it to your parents. a. b.
6. Don't tell us to hurry. a. b.

FIGURE IT OUT

Which intonation pattern do you hear in statements and commands? Write a rule.

RULE FOR STATEMENTS AND COMMANDS

Statements and commands use *(circle one)*   rising/falling   rising   intonation.

Now listen to the statements and commands again and repeat them. The last word in each has two syllables. Where does the tone rise? Where does the tone fall? Write a rule.

RULE FOR RISING AND FALLING TONES

The tone rises on the _____ stressed syllable of a sentence. The tone falls after the _____ stressed syllable of a sentence.

LISTENING

Now listen to these statements and commands with stress on the *last* syllable.

1. I wasn't able to cash a check.
2. He doesn't know how to spell your name.
3. June twenty-fourth is the first day of class.
4. Please lock the door when you leave.
5. Bring your notes for the test.
6. Don't forget to write the date.

When the last stress is the *last* syllable, make the tone *rise* and *fall* on the *same* syllable.

1. SPEAKING. Guided Conversation to Practice Rising/Falling Intonation.

DIRECTIONS: Here is a list of topics. With a partner, take turns expressing your opinions and agreeing or disagreeing. Use rising/falling intonation in your statements.

EXAMPLE:

STUDENT 1:   I believe the best <u>time to exercise</u> is early in the morning.

STUDENT 2:   I couldn't agree more. I think the best <u>sport</u> is soccer.

STUDENT 1:   Oh, I'm not so sure. I believe the best <u>sport</u> is . . .

TOPICS

car	sport
tourist site	job
time to study	TV program
kind of dessert	way to travel
climate	place to have fun
time to exercise	American city

PARTNER 1

2a. LISTENING DISCRIMINATION AND SPEAKING. Mystery Drawing. Pair Practice for Rising/Falling Intonation in Commands. PARTNER 1. Use this page. PARTNER 2. Turn to page 74.

DIRECTIONS: Below you see two drawings. First, tell your partner how to make each one. Use rising/falling intonation in your commands.

EXAMPLE:
YOU: For the first one, make a large circle. Then draw a . . .

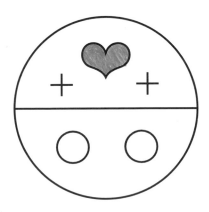 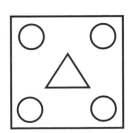 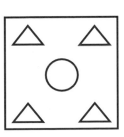

Now get a pencil and paper and listen. Your partner will tell you how to make two different drawings.
Now compare drawings with your partner.

3a. LISTENING DISCRIMINATION AND SPEAKING. Opposites. Class Game for Rising/Falling Intonation in Statements.   TEAM 1. Use this page. TEAM 2. Turn to page 74.

DIRECTIONS: First, take turns with other students on your team. Make one of the statements below to Team 2. Then Team 2 must respond with a statement that means the *opposite* of your team's statement. Team 2 gets one point for each correct response.

EXAMPLE:

TEAM 1: His clothing was <u>casual</u>.

TEAM 2: That's not true. His clothing was <u>formal</u>. (1 point)

1. The movie's going to be dull.
2. This weather's unbearable.
3. She's quite optimistic.
4. The play's going to be a comedy.
5. The price of gold will fall.
6. She's very clumsy.
7. The experiment's been a success.

Now listen to Team 2's statements and take turns responding. Your responses must mean the *opposite* of Team 2's statements. Your team gets one point for each correct response.

EXAMPLE:

TEAM 2: She was recently <u>fired</u>.

TEAM 1: That's not true. She was recently <u>hired</u>. (1 point)

Now compare scores. Which team knew the most opposites? Congratulations!

4. SPEAKING. Witness. Pair Practice for Rising/Falling Intonation in Statements.

DIRECTIONS: Your instructor will give you and your partner a picture. The two of you should study it for two minutes. Then *only* Student 1 looks at the picture while Student 2 describes it in as much detail as possible. At the end of the description, Student 1 adds any details missing. When you are finished, tell your instructor. You will be given a second picture to repeat the practice; Students 1 and 2 should change roles.

5. REPORT. Memorable Event.

DIRECTIONS: Prepare a three- to five-minute report on something you have experienced that will interest the rest of the class. Here are some possible topics:

a. a recurring dream
b. a sports event
c. an unusual film
d. a wonderful place
e. a strange incident

PART TWO Questions with *wh-* Words

Questions beginning with *wh-* words ask for information as an answer. How many *wh-* words do you know? Write them here:

_____

_____

Do your classmates know others? Write any others with yours.

In Lesson 6, you learned about stress in *wh-* questions. Now you will learn about *wh-* question intonation.

LISTENING DISCRIMINATION.

DIRECTIONS: Listen to these *wh-* questions. Circle the letter of the intonation you hear.

EXAMPLE: Where are you going? (a.) b.

1. How many people are coming? a. b.
2. When will they finish? a. b.
3. What did you copy? a. b.

4. Who's able to answer? a. b.
5. Why was it damaged? a. b.
6. How have you been feeling? a. b.

FIGURE IT OUT

Which intonation pattern do you hear in *wh-* questions? Write a rule.

RULE FOR *WH-* QUESTIONS

Wh- questions use *(circle one)*   rising/falling   rising   intonation.

Now listen to the *wh-* questions again and repeat them. The last word in each has two syllables. Their intonation is similar to statements and commands. Tone rises on the last stressed syllable of the question and then falls for all following syllables.

When the last stress is the *last* syllable, make the tone *rise* and *fall* on the *same* syllable.

Listen to and repeat these examples:

Where have you been?

What time does it start?

Why did it take so long?

How much does it cost?

Who won the game?

When's the test?

PRACTICE ACTIVITIES

1. SPEAKING. American Magazines. Guided Conversation to Practice Rising/Falling Intonation in *wh-* Questions.

DIRECTIONS: Here are lists of magazines and topics. With a partner, take turns asking and answering questions. Use rising/falling intonation in your *wh-* questions.

EXAMPLE:

STUDENT 1:   What do you think of the latest issue of *Time*?

STUDENT 2:   It's fantastic. How often do you buy it?

STUDENT 1:   All the time! It's one of the best <u>news</u> magazines in America.

MAGAZINES		TOPICS
Better Homes and Gardens	*TV Guide*	beauty
Car and Driver	*Glamour*	<u>car</u>
Field and Stream	*Vogue*	exercise
Good Housekeeping		fashion
U.S. News and World Report		fishing
Newsweek		health
Prevention		home improvement
Shape		news
Sports Illustrated		sports
Time		TV

2a. SPEAKING AND LISTENING. Pair Practice for Rising/Falling Intonation in *wh-* Questions. PARTNER 1. Use this page. PARTNER 2. Turn to page 75.

DIRECTIONS: Below you see a chart of information about inventions. Take turns asking and answering *who* and *when* questions about them. Write the answers on the chart. Use rising/falling intonation in your questions and answers.

EXAMPLE:

YOU: Who invented the television?

YOUR PARTNER: John Baird.

YOU: When was it invented?

YOUR PARTNER: 1926. Who invented the phonograph?

Invention	Inventor	Year
The vacuum cleaner	Hubert Booth	1901
The telephone	_____	_____
The photocopy machine	Chester Carlson	1940
The elevator	_____	_____
The alarm clock	Levi Hutchins	1787
The washing machine	_____	_____
Dynamite	Alfred Nobel	1866
The Model T car	_____	_____
The rubber band	_____	_____
Frozen food	Clarence Birdseye	1925
The television	*John Baird*	*1926*
The phonograph	Thomas Edison	1877
The typewriter	Christopher Sholes	1873
The ballpoint pen	Biro brothers	1938
The telegraph	_____	_____
The tire	_____	_____

Now compare answers with your partner.

3a. LISTENING DISCRIMINATION AND SPEAKING. Think Fast. Pair Practice for Rising/Falling Intonation in *wh-* Questions and Statements. PARTNER 1. Use this page. PARTNER 2. Turn to page 76.

DIRECTIONS: Here are some imaginary events. First, ask what your partner's reaction would be if these events happened. Use *wh-* questions with *would*.

EXAMPLES:

YOU: Suppose a fire started right now. Where would you go?

YOUR PARTNER: I'd go out of the building.

YOU: Suppose you broke a friend's TV. What would you say?

YOUR PARTNER: I'd say I'm sorry.

Suppose . . .

1. you found a hundred-dollar bill.
2. you met the President of the United States.
3. you were late for an important test.
4. you had to give a speech right now.
5. you didn't understand the instructor's question.
6. a famous movie star called you for a date.

Now your partner's going to ask you some questions about imaginary events. Create your own answers with *I'd*. Use rising/falling intonation.

4. INTERVIEW AND REPORT. Birthday Gift. Small Group Practice for Rising/Falling Intonation in *wh-* Questions and Statements.

DIRECTIONS: Each person in your group should choose one of the three roles:

STUDENT 1:   Interview Student 2 about favorite things and preferences. You can use the topics below or create your own questions.

STUDENT 2:   Answer Student 1's questions.

STUDENT 3:   Observe the interview and take notes. At the end of the interview, use information about Student 2's likes and preferences to suggest a good birthday gift.

At the end of the interview, change roles. Then change roles again until all three students have a suggested gift. After the interviews, report to the class about your suggested birthday gift and why you believe it is a good choice.

POSSIBLE QUESTION TOPICS

What's your favorite . . . ?	What kinds of . . . do you like?
color	TV programs
sport	movies
free-time activity	music
academic subject	magazines
hobby	restaurants
game	clothing
food	

You learned about **focus** in Lesson 6. Do you remember some reasons why speakers sometimes use focus?

When speakers say a focus word or syllable longer and louder than all other syllables in a sentence, they can also use *extra high* intonation. Tone is then low for all syllables after the focus word.

 Listen to these examples:

It was the last day of class.

We had a wonderful time.

I got an A, and Sheila got a C.

She enjoys being a car mechanic.

Speakers use extra high intonation with focus to express very strong emphasis or emotions like excitement, happiness, anger, and shock.

PRACTICE ACTIVITIES

1. SPEAKING. Guided Conversation to Practice Rising/Falling Intonation and Focus.

DIRECTIONS: Study the example conversation. Use the example and list of adjectives to create conversations with a partner. Use extra high intonation and focus for strong emphasis and emotion.

    EXAMPLE:

STUDENT 1: That party was pretty dull.

STUDENT 2: I don't think it was dull. In fact, it was exciting. I had a good time!

STUDENT 1: Well, I'm glad somebody enjoyed it.

ADJECTIVES

tame / wild
boring / interesting
dull / exciting
low-key / upbeat
tiring / stimulating
dreary / lively
terrible / terrific
stale / refreshing

2a. LISTENING DISCRIMINATION AND SPEAKING. Pair Practice for Rising/Falling Intonation and Focus.   PARTNER 1. Use this page. PARTNER 2. Turn to page 77.

DIRECTIONS: First, say the sentences below to your partner. Your partner will respond with emotional focus. Show your own happiness or sadness with a follow-up remark. Study these examples:

YOU: I got fired from my job.

YOUR PARTNER: That's terrible news! I'm so sorry to hear it.

YOU: Me too. I'm really upset about it.

YOU: I finally got a new car.

YOUR PARTNER: That's wonderful news! I'm so glad to hear it.

YOU: Me too. I'm really happy about it.

1.   I got accepted to graduate school.
2.   I found a beautiful apartment to rent.
3.   My dog ran away.
4.   I flunked the midterm exam.
5.   Somebody slashed my tires.
6.   My financial aid loan was approved.

Now your partner's going to tell you some good and bad news. Listen and respond with emotional focus. You can use the expressions below or create your own.

EXPRESSIONS

That's . . . news. I'm so . . . to hear it.
wonderful / glad
fantastic / happy
great / thrilled
horrible / sad
terrible /sorry
awful / shocked

3. REPORT. Small Group Practice for Rising/Falling Intonation and Focus.

DIRECTIONS: Take turns with other students in your group telling a two- to four-minute story about something exciting, shocking, sad, frustrating, or wonderful that has happened to you. At the end of each story, listeners should comment with emotional focus.

2b. LISTENING DISCRIMINATION AND SPEAKING. Mystery Drawing. Pair Practice for Rising/Falling Intonation in Commands. PARTNER 2. Use this page. PARTNER 1. Turn to page 67.

DIRECTIONS: You and your partner each have different drawings. First, get a pencil and paper and listen. Your partner will tell you how to make two drawings. Below you see two drawings. Now, tell your partner how to make each one. Use rising/falling intonation in your commands.

EXAMPLE:
YOU: For the first one, make a large square. Then draw a . . .

 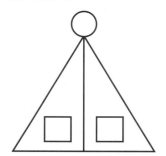

Now compare drawings with your partner.

3b. LISTENING DISCRIMINATION AND SPEAKING. Opposites. Class Game for Rising/Falling Intonation in Statements. TEAM 2. Use this page. TEAM 1. Turn to page 68.

DIRECTIONS: First, listen to Team 1's statements and take turns responding. Your responses must mean the *opposite* of Team 1's statements. Your team gets one point for each correct response.

EXAMPLE:

TEAM 1: His clothing was <u>casual</u>.

TEAM 2: That's not true. His clothing was <u>formal</u>. (1 point)

Now take turns with other students on your team. Make one of the statements below to Team 1. Then Team 1 must respond with a statement that means the *opposite* of your team's statement. Team 1 gets one point for each correct response.

EXAMPLE:

TEAM 2: She was recently <u>fired</u>.

TEAM 1: That's not true. She was recently <u>hired</u>. (1 point)

8. He's ordered his steak well-done.
9. Crime is decreasing.
10. Bob was talking to the guest.
11. The rewards will be enormous.
12. The directions are simple.
13. The bread was stale.
14. They're learning gradually.

Now compare scores. Which team knew the most opposites? Congratulations!

PAIR PRACTICE: Partner 2

2b. SPEAKING AND LISTENING. Pair Practice for Rising/Falling Intonation in *wh-*Questions. PARTNER 2. Use this page. PARTNER 1. Turn to page 70.

DIRECTIONS: Below you see a chart of information about inventions. Take turns asking and answering *who* and *when* questions about them. Write the answers on the chart. Use rising/falling intonation in your questions and answers.

EXAMPLE:

YOU: Who invented the phonograph?

YOUR PARTNER: Thomas Edison.

YOU: When was it invented?

YOUR PARTNER: 1877. Who invented the television?

Invention	Inventor	Year
The vacuum cleaner		
The telephone	Alexander Bell	1876
The photocopy machine		
The elevator	Elisha Otis	1850
The alarm clock		
The washing machine	Alva Fisher	1910
Dynamite		
The Model T car	Henry Ford	1908
The rubber band	Thomas Hancock	1820
Frozen food		
The television	John Baird	1926
The phonograph	*Thomas Edison*	*1877*
The typewriter		
The ballpoint pen		
The telegraph	Samuel Morse	1837
The tire	John Dunlop	1888

Now compare answers with your partner.

PAIR PRACTICE: Partner 2

3b. LISTENING DISCRIMINATION AND SPEAKING. Think Fast. Pair Practice for Rising/Falling Intonation in *wh-* Questions and Statements. PARTNER 2. Use this page. PARTNER 1. Turn to page 71.

DIRECTIONS: First, your partner's going to ask you some questions about imaginary events. Create your own answers with *I'd*. Use rising/falling intonation.

EXAMPLES:

YOUR PARTNER: Suppose a fire started right now. Where would you go?

YOU: I'd go out of the building.

YOUR PARTNER: Suppose you broke a friend's TV. What would you say?

YOU: I'd say I'm sorry.

Here are some imaginary events. Now ask what your partner's reaction would be if these events happened. Use *wh-* questions with *would*.

Suppose . . .

1. you lost your wallet.

2. the phone company cut off your service.

3. you ran out of money on a vacation.

4. you found an unlimited plane ticket.

5. you inherited your family's business.

6. your instructor announced a pop quiz right now.

PAIR PRACTICE: Partner 2

2b. LISTENING DISCRIMINATION AND SPEAKING. Pair Practice for Rising/Falling Intonation and Focus. PARTNER 2. Use this page. PARTNER 1. Turn to page 73.

DIRECTIONS: First, your partner's going to tell you some good and bad news. Listen and respond with emotional focus. You can use the expressions below or create your own.

EXAMPLES:

YOUR PARTNER: I got fired from my job.

YOU: That's terrible news! I'm so sorry to hear it.

YOUR PARTNER: Me too. I'm really upset about it.

YOUR PARTNER: I finally got a new car.

YOU: That's wonderful news! I'm so glad to hear it.

YOUR PARTNER: Me too. I'm really happy about it.

EXPRESSIONS

That's . . . news. I'm so . . . to hear it.
wonderful / glad
fantastic / happy
great / thrilled
horrible / sad
terrible / sorry
awful / shocked

Now say the sentences below to your partner. Your partner will respond with emotional focus. Show your own happiness or sadness with a follow-up remark. Study the examples above.

1. My boyfriend/girlfriend and I broke up last night.
2. I got a promotion.
3. Somebody stole my car stereo.
4. I got straight A's.
5. I lost my checkbook this morning.
6. The committee gave me a scholarship.

Rising Intonation

In Lesson 8, you learned about three tones in English intonation. You also learned that there are basically two intonation patterns in English: *rising/falling* and *rising*. Statements, commands, and questions with *wh-* words all use rising/falling intonation. Questions with *yes* or *no* for answers use *rising* intonation. This lesson is about *rising* intonation and *yes/no* questions.

Here is the example yes/no question you have already seen:

high	_____ leaving?
medium	_____ Are they _____
low	_____

The question starts on the medium tone. Then it rises to the high tone. This is a *rising* intonation. This book shows *rising* intonation like this:

Is she going?   Do we finish at one?

Yes/no questions can be negative or affirmative. Look at and listen to these examples:

Did they meet you at the airport? (affirmative question)
Won't we get a refund? (negative question)

LISTENING

Listen to these *yes/no* questions with stress on the last syllable.

1. Wasn't his voice soft?
2. Did you finally get a job?
3. Hasn't she finished yet?
4. Had they already called?
5. Don't we need our books?
6. Will I see you in class?

FIGURE IT OUT

Now listen to the *yes/no* questions again and repeat them. The last stressed word in each question has one syllable. Where does the tone rise? Write a rule.

RULE FOR RISING TONE

The tone rises on the _____ stressed syllable of a yes/no question.

LISTENING

Listen to these yes/no questions. They do not have stress on the last syllable.

1. Can you play tennis?
2. Has he ever gone to college?
3. Wouldn't she be interested?
4. Should we meet tomorrow?
5. Weren't the tests easy?
6. Are you coming to the concert?

There are one or more unstressed syllables after the last sentence stress. Make the tone rise on the last stress. Continue on the high tone to the end of the *yes/no* question.

Now listen to the *yes/no* questions again and repeat them. Practice rising to and staying on the high tone.

PRACTICE ACTIVITIES

1. SPEAKING AND LISTENING. Find Someone. Class Practice for Rising Intonation.

DIRECTIONS: All class members should stand up and ask others about the activities on the list below. Put the name of any class member who answers *yes* after each activity. Continue to ask different students *yes/no* questions until you have as many names on the list as possible. Use rising intonation.

EXAMPLE:

YOU: Joe, do you have a pet?

JOE: Yes, I have a cat.

Find someone who . . . <u>has a pet</u>.   <u>   Joe   </u>

Find someone who . . .

1. speaks three languages.   _____
2. has more than one brother.   _____
3. plays golf.   _____
4. can type faster than 55 words per minute. _____
5. likes horror movies.   _____
6. owns two watches.   _____
7. has visited Disneyland.   _____
8. used to take piano lessons.   _____
9. has a birthday this month.   _____
10. lives with a family member.   _____
11. never drinks coffee.   _____
12. is an only child.   _____

2a. LISTENING DISCRIMINATION AND SPEAKING. Offers. Pair Practice for Rising Intonation.   PARTNER 1. Use this page. PARTNER 2. Turn to page 83.

DIRECTIONS: Make the statements below. Your partner will respond with an offer. Create your own acceptance or refusal of the offer.

EXAMPLE:

YOU: It's hot in here.

YOUR PARTNER: Do you want me to open the window?

YOU: Yes, that'd be great.

1. I'm thirsty.
2. I can't hear you.
3. My hair is messy.
4. I need to look up a word.

5. This suitcase's awfully heavy.
6. I can't find Mason Street.
7. The door's locked.
8. My tire's flat.

Now listen carefully to your partner's statements. Create a *yes/no* question offer in response to each one. You can use *do you want me to*, *should I*, *can I*, or any other phrases you know.

EXAMPLE:

YOUR PARTNER: I'm hungry.

YOU: Should I make a sandwich for you?

YOUR PARTNER: Oh, no thanks. I'll wait till I get home.

3. SPEAKING. Not Yes, Not No. Class Game to Practice Rising Intonation.

DIRECTIONS: Your instructor will divide you into Team 1 and Team 2. First, Team 1 members will create their own *yes/no* questions and take turns asking Team 2. Your instructor will tell you how many questions to create. Team 2 *must* answer with one of the expressions below. If they say *yes* or *no*, they get one point.

At the end of the round, change roles. Team 2 will ask yes/no questions and Team 1 will answer. The winning team is the one with the *lowest* score. Study the example:

EXAMPLE:

TEAM 1:   Marta, are you married?

MARTA (TEAM 2):   Certainly not.

TEAM 1:   Ivan, are you good at math?

IVAN (TEAM 2):   You bet.

TEAM 1:   Nori, do you know how to swim?

NORI (TEAM 2):   Yes, of course. (1 point)

EXPRESSIONS FOR YES

Of course.   Certainly.   By all means.   You bet.   Sure.

EXPRESSIONS FOR NO

Absolutely not.   Not really.   Of course not.   Certainly not.   Not at all.

Which team had the lowest score? Congratulations!

4. SPEAKING. One-Way Dialogs. Pair Practice for Rising and Rising/Falling Intonation.

DIRECTIONS: With a partner, study the dialogs below. Create the missing parts of each dialog. When you are finished, choose which partner will be A and which will be B. Then read your dialogs aloud to the class. Use rising/falling intonation for statements, commands, and *wh-* questions. Use rising intonation for yes/no questions.

EXAMPLE:

A: Are you going to the gym?

B: *Not today.*

A: Well, how about tomorrow?

B: *Maybe in the morning.*

1. A: Have you seen Donna?

   B:

   A: She dyed her hair red!

   B:

2. A: Have you already bought tickets?

   B:

   A: When do you plan to go?

   B:

3. A: Would you like a Coke?

   B:

   A: OK. Are you hungry?

   B:

4. A: Was that phone call for me?

   B:

   A: If Jason calls, can you take a message?

   B:

5. A: Are you lost?

   B:

   A: It's just a block from here on the left.

   B:

6. A:

   B: Not today.

   A:

   B: That would be fun.

7. A:

   B: Am I late?

   A:

   B: I'm sorry.

8. A:

   B: Yes, she told me last night.

   A:

   B: I know. I think she's crazy!

9. A:

   B: No problem. It's easy.

   A:

   B: Don't mention it.

10. A:

    B: No, not yet.

    A:

    B: Maybe later.

5. INTERVIEW. Pair Practice to Contrast Rising and Rising/Falling Intonation.

DIRECTIONS: Interview a partner about possessions. Your partner will interview you, too. Choose who will ask or answer first. Use the cues to ask *yes/no* questions and *wh-* questions with *what kind of*.

EXAMPLE:

(cue) . . . stereo system?

YOU: Do you have a stereo system?

YOUR PARTNER: Yes.

YOU: What kind of stereo system do you have?

YOUR PARTNER: It's a Sony.

Take notes to help you remember your partner's answers. After the interview, tell the class about your partner's possessions.

CUES

1. . . . TV?   6. . . . watch?
2. . . . car?   7. . . . bike?
3. . . . dictionary?   8. . . . camera?
4. . . . computer?   9. . . . typewriter?
5. . . . calculator?   10. . . . CD player?

6. REPORT. Amazing But True. Small Group Practice to Contrast Rising and Rising/Falling Intonation.

DIRECTIONS: Ask other members of your group about the unusual events below. Choose one member's *yes* answer and ask questions with *wh-* words to get details about the event. Take notes and prepare a three- to five-minute report about a classmate's unusual experience. Each member of your group should report on a different classmate.

Have you ever . . .

1. met a famous person?
2. won a prize?
3. gotten straight A's?
4. ridden in a limousine?
5. found a lot of money?
6. seen an eclipse?
7. saved someone's life?
8. seen a UFO?

2b. LISTENING DISCRIMINATION AND SPEAKING. Offers. Pair Practice for Rising Intonation. PARTNER 2. Use this page. PARTNER 1. Turn to page 80.

DIRECTIONS: Listen carefully to your partner's statements. Create a yes/no question offer in response to each one. You can use *do you want me to, should I, can I*, or any other phrases you know.

EXAMPLE:

YOUR PARTNER: It's hot in here.

YOU: Do you want me to open the window?

YOUR PARTNER: Yes, that'd be great.

Now make the statements below. Your partner will respond with an offer. Create your own acceptance or refusal of the offer.

EXAMPLE:

YOU: I'm hungry.

YOUR PARTNER: Should I make a sandwich for you?

YOU: Oh, no thanks. I'll wait till I get home.

1. My pencil is broken.
2. I'm chilly.
3. My car won't start.
4. I've aleady seen this TV show.
5. I can't get this math problem right.
6. My watch has stopped.
7. I need to make a phone call.
8. I have a headache.

Combination Intonation Patterns

In Lessons 8 and 9, you learned about and practiced two basic intonation patterns. This lesson is about sentences and questions that have both *rising/falling* and *rising* intonation.

PART ONE   Questions with *or*

PRACTICE ACTIVITIES

 1. LISTENING.

DIRECTIONS: Here are some questions with the word *or*. They ask the listener to choose *one* of *two* choices. Listen to the underlined words in each question.

1. Do you want <u>ham</u> or <u>cheese</u>?	5. Would you like <u>nonfat</u> or <u>whole</u> milk?
2. Did he take <u>algebra</u> or <u>geometry</u>?	6. Has he been at <u>home</u> or at <u>work</u>?
3. Will she call <u>Thursday</u> or <u>Friday</u>?	7. Can we <u>rent</u> it or <u>buy</u> it?
4. Are you paying by <u>check</u> or in <u>cash</u>?	8. Did they see it on <u>TV</u> or at the <u>movies</u>?

FIGURE IT OUT

Each question has two underlined choice words. What intonation pattern do you hear for the choice words? Write a rule.

RULE FOR CHOICE QUESTIONS WITH *OR*

For *or* questions that ask for a choice, the first choice word has _____
intonation, and the second choice word has _____ intonation.

2. READ ALOUD AND ANSWER.

DIRECTIONS: Now take turns reading the above choice questions to a partner. You or your partner should answer by choosing *one* of the choice words.

> **EXAMPLE:**
> STUDENT 1: Do you want ham or cheese?
> STUDENT 2: I'll have cheese.

3. LISTENING.

DIRECTIONS: Here are some *yes/no* questions with *or*. Some of them make an offer. Listen to the two underlined words in each question.

1. Would you like coffee or tea?
2. Did he go to high school or college?
3. Do you need a pencil or pen?
4. Is there something to eat or drink?
5. Do you want a spoon or fork?
6. Will you buy a bike or car?
7. Were they upset or angry?
8. Would you like some ice or a straw?

FIGURE IT OUT

Each *yes/no* question with *or* has two underlined words. What intonation pattern do you hear for both words? Write a rule.

RULE FOR YES/NO QUESTIONS WITH *OR*

For *or* questions that ask for *yes* or *no,* both words have _____ intonation.

4. READ ALOUD AND ANSWER.

DIRECTIONS: Now take turns reading the above *yes/no* questions and offers with *or* to a partner. You or your partner should answer "*yes*" or "*no*" for *yes/no* questions. Answer "*Yes, please*" or "*No, thanks*" for offers.

> **EXAMPLE:**
> STUDENT 1: Would you like coffee or tea?
> STUDENT 2: No, thanks.

5. READ ALOUD.

DIRECTIONS: First look at the answers to these questions with *or*. Then ask the questions and intone them correctly.

> **EXAMPLE:**
> Did you come to class on time or late? (On time, as usual.)

1. Would you like juice or milk? (I'll take milk.)
2. Do you want to watch TV or a movie? (No. I'm going to bed.)
3. Does he play the piano or violin? (Yes, he plays both.)
4. Are we eating out or at home? (Let's eat out.)
5. Do you want cream or sugar? (No, thanks.)
6. Is his shirt red or orange? (I think it's orange.)
7. Are you hungry or thirsty? (No, not really.)
8. Have you been swimming or sailing? (Sailing.)
9. Should we have fruit or ice cream? (Fruit is better.)
10. Did they order fish or chicken? (No, neither one.)
11. Is he studying medicine or engineering? (Medicine.)
12. Is the meeting Monday or Friday? (Friday at 2 o'clock.)

6. SPEAKING. Guided Conversation to Practice Choice Questions with *or*.

DIRECTIONS: Here are lists of food and drinks. With a partner, take turns being the host and the guest. Intone your questions correctly.

EXAMPLE:

HOST: Would you like some ice cream?

GUEST: Yes, I sure would.

HOST: Do you want chocolate or vanilla?

GUEST: I'll have chocolate.

FOOD

fruit / melon / grapes
ice cream / chocolate / vanilla
bread / white / wheat
turkey / white meat / dark meat
potatoes / baked / mashed
rice / white / brown
soup / tomato / noodle
chicken / a leg / a wing
olives / black / green

DRINKS

coffee / espresso / regular
wine / red / white
juice / orange / apple
tea / iced / hot
beer / light / dark
milk / whole / low-fat
Coke / diet / regular

PARTNER 1

7a. LISTENING DISCRIMINATION AND SPEAKING. Pair Practice for Questions with *or*.   PARTNER 1. Use this page. PARTNER 2. Turn to page 90.

DIRECTIONS: Ask your partner the following questions and intone them as marked. The correct answers are in parentheses ( ). If your partner gives an incorrect answer, repeat your question. Be sure to intone the question as marked.

1. Would you care for a Coke or a Dr. Pepper? (Yes, please.)

2. Did you find this book at the library or the bookstore? (At the library.)

3. Will he buy a motorcycle or a scooter? (A scooter, I think.)

4. Do you like cherries or peaches? (No, I never eat fruit.)

5. Is this the first time or the second? (It's the second.)

6. Do you need a rake or a hoe? (Yes. Thanks for the offer.)

7. Was she talking or laughing? (No. She was very quiet.)

8. Does the movie start this weekend or next? (This weekend.)

9. Should we buy a house or condo? (No, I don't think so.)

10. Is she your daughter or your niece? (She's my daughter.)

Now your partner will ask some questions. Listen to intonation. Answer with a choice if you hear a choice question. Answer with *yes* or *no* if you hear a *yes/no* question with *or*.

1. At the office.	No, he didn't.
2. A pen please.	No. I have a pen.
3. Orange.	Yes, it's lemon.
4. At five.	No. Not till much later.
5. A hotel.	Yes, we did.
6. Tall.	No. Short and fat.
7. It was windy.	Yes. Very unpleasant.
8. Two fives, please.	No. I already have change.
9. Write about it.	Yes, do both.
10. I'll have chicken.	No. I'm a vegetarian.

8. INTERVIEW. Preferences. Pair Practice for Intonation of Questions with *or*.

DIRECTIONS: Interview a partner about her/his preferences. You can use the categories in the cues below to form questions, or you can create your own. Take notes to help you remember your partner's answers. Your partner will interview you, too. Choose who will ask or answer first. After the interviews, use your notes to tell the class about your partner.

EXAMPLE: (cue) sports (individual / team)

YOU: Do you like individual sports or team sports?

YOUR PARTNER: Team sports.

CUES

1. books (fiction / nonfiction)
2. movies (action / romantic)
3. clothes (casual / dressy)
4. cars (economy / luxury)

5. sports (individual / team)
6. classes (science / art)
7. music (rock / classical)
8. food (spicy / bland)

PART TWO   Listing with *and* and *or*

PRACTICE ACTIVITIES

 1. LISTENING.

DIRECTIONS: Here are some sentences and questions with **listing**. Each list has two or more items. Listen to the underlined words in each list.

1. Our class meets Monday, Wednesday, and Friday.
2. She can speak, read, and write English.
3. The machine takes nickels or dimes.
4. Has it been easy, average, or difficult?
5. The odd numbers were seven, nine, and eleven.
6. He designed it, built it, and lived in it.
7. Will you drop by, write, or phone?
8. She answered quickly and softly.

FIGURE IT OUT

What intonation pattern do you hear for listing? Write a rule.

RULE FOR LISTING WITH *AND* AND *OR*

For sentences and questions with lists joined by *and* and *or,* each member of the list has _____ intonation, and the last member has _____ intonation.

2. PRACTICE.

DIRECTIONS: Now listen to and repeat the listing sentences and questions.

3. SPEAKING. Common Denominators. Class Game to Practice Listing Intonation.

DIRECTIONS: Here are twenty boxes with a picture of an object in each one. Your instructor will ask you some questions. Respond with the names of all objects that can answer the questions. Use listing intonation.

EXAMPLE:

INSTRUCTOR: Which ones can you wear?

STUDENT: Shoes, a hat, and a jacket.

4a. LISTENING DISCRIMINATION AND SPEAKING. Odd One Out. Pair Practice for Listing Intonation. PARTNER 1. Use this page. PARTNER 2. Turn to page 91.

DIRECTIONS: You have groups of four words below. One underlined word in each group does not belong. First, say each group of words to your partner. Use listing intonation. Your partner will choose the *one* word that is the "odd one out." Repeat the group if your partner answers incorrectly.

> **EXAMPLE:**
> YOU: Purple, heavy, violet, and yellow.
> YOUR PARTNER: Heavy.

1. crow, robin, cobra, eagle
2. silver, ruby, diamond, emerald
3. ocean, sea, desert, river
4. piano, cello, violin, compass
5. pour, bake, boil, fry
6. sand, gold, steel, iron
7. brain, heart, head, lungs
8. tennis, badminton, ping-pong, hockey

Now your partner will say some groups of four words. *One* word in each group does not belong. Listen and say the word that is the "odd one out." Your partner will repeat if you answer incorrectly.

> **EXAMPLE:**
> YOUR PARTNER: String, rope, glue, thread.
> YOU: Glue.

5a. LISTENING DISCRIMINATION and Speaking. Name Three Things. Class Game to Practice Listing Intonation. TEAM 1. Use this page. TEAM 2. Turn to page 92.

DIRECTIONS: First, choose a speaker to say Cue 1 below to Team 2. Team 2 will try to name three things in response to the cue. They get one point for each correct response. Your instructor will keep score. Choose a different speaker for each cue. Study this example:

> TEAM 1 FIRST SPEAKER: Name three vegetables that begin with the letter C.
>
> TEAM 2 FIRST SPEAKER: Carrots, cabbage, and corn. (3 points)

1. Name three parts of the body that begin with the letter H.
2. Name three countries that begin with the letter B.
3. Name three fruits that begin with the letter P.
4. Name three academic subjects that begin with the letter E.
5. Name three sports that begin with the letter S.
6. Name three continents that begin with the letter A.
7. Name three U.S. states that begin with the letter M.
8. Name three types of music that begin with the letter R.

Now Team 2 is going to say some cues to your team. Choose a speaker for each cue before you hear it. Then your team has 15 seconds to agree on three things in response to each cue and have the speaker say your team's responses. The speaker needs to use listing intonation in the response. Your instructor will continue to keep score. Each correct response is worth one point.

> **EXAMPLE:**
>
> TEAM 2 FIRST SPEAKER: Name three colors that begin with the letter G.
>
> TEAM 1 FIRST SPEAKER: Gray, green, and gold. (3 points)

Which team had the highest score? Congratulations!

6. DISCUSS AND REPORT. Small Group Practice for Listing Intonation.

DIRECTIONS: You and your group need to choose two of the topics. Discuss them and reach an agreement with your group. Then have different group members tell the class the results of your discussion.

TOPICS

A. Where are the three best places to do homework? Why? Where are the three worse places? Why?

B. What are the four most important things a person should bring when taking a vacation in a foreign country? Why is each thing important?

C. What are the four most important skills a person should have to get by in life? What is someone able to do with each skill?

D. Where are the three most interesting places to visit in the world? What makes each place interesting?

PARTNER 2

7b. LISTENING DISCRIMINATION AND SPEAKING. Pair Practice for Questions with *or*. PARTNER 2. Use this page. PARTNER 1. Turn to page 86.

DIRECTIONS: Your partner will ask some questions with *or*. Listen to intonation. Answer with a choice if you hear a choice question. Answer with *yes* or *no* if you hear a *yes/no* question with *or*.

1. I'll have Coke thanks.	Yes, please.
2. At the library.	No, I didn't.
3. A scooter, I think.	Yes, he eventually will.
4. I prefer cherries.	No, I never eat fruit.
5. It's the second.	Yes, it is.
6. I need a hoe.	Yes. Thanks for the offer.
7. Talking.	No. She was very quiet.
8. This weekend.	Yes, very soon.
9. A house would be better.	No, I don't think so.
10. She's my daughter.	No. A neighbor.

Now ask your partner the following questions and intone them as marked. The correct answers are in parentheses ( ). If your partner gives an incorrect answer, repeat your question. Be sure to intone the question as marked.

1. Did he work at home or at the office? (At the office.)

2. Would you like a pen or pencil? (No. I have a pen.)

3. Is this ice cream lemon or orange? (Yes, it's lemon.)

4. Will you be home at five or six? (At five.)

5. Did you stay in a hotel or a motel? (A hotel.)

6. Was the man tall or thin? (No. Short and fat.)

7. Was the weather cold or windy? (Yes. Very unpleasant.)

8. Do you want two five-dollar bills or a ten? (Two fives, please.)

9. Should we write about it or talk about it? (Yes. Do both.)

10. Will you order beef or chicken? (I'll have chicken.)

4b. LISTENING DISCRIMINATION AND SPEAKING. Odd One Out. Pair Practice for Listing Intonation.   PARTNER 2. Use this page. PARTNER 1. Turn to page 89.

DIRECTIONS: First, your partner will say some groups of four words. *One* word in each group does not belong. Listen and say the word that is the "odd one out." Your partner will repeat if you answer incorrectly.

> **EXAMPLE:**
> YOUR PARTNER: Purple, <u>heavy</u>, violet, and yellow.
> YOU: Heavy.

Now you have groups of four words below. One <u>underlined</u> word in each group does not belong. Say each group of words to your partner. Use listing intonation. Your partner will choose the *one* word that is the "odd one out." Repeat the group if your partner answers incorrectly.

> **EXAMPLE:**
> YOU: String, rope, <u>glue</u>, thread.
> YOUR PARTNER: Glue.

1. <u>pine</u>, cotton, silk, wool
2. chat, <u>laugh</u>, talk, speak
3. sailing, surfing, <u>hunting</u>, diving
4. slippers, boots, sandals, <u>gloves</u>
5. <u>thunder</u>, earthquake, flood, hurricane
6. <u>run</u>, drive, ride, fly
7. period, comma, <u>sentence</u>, question mark
8. block, cube, box, <u>ball</u>

PAIR PRACTICE: Partner 2

5b. LISTENING DISCRIMINATION AND SPEAKING. Name Three Things. Class Game to Practice Listing Intonation. TEAM 2. Use this page. TEAM 1. Turn to page 89.

DIRECTIONS: First, Team 1 is going to say some cues to your team. Choose a speaker for each cue before you hear it. Then your team has 15 seconds to agree on three things in response to each cue and have the speaker say your team's responses. The speaker needs to use listing intonation in the response. Your instructor will keep score. Each correct response is worth one point. Study this example:

> TEAM 1 FIRST SPEAKER: Name three vegetables that begin with the letter C.
>
> TEAM 2 FIRST SPEAKER: Carrots, cabbage, and corn. (3 points)

Now choose a speaker to say Cue 1 below to Team 1. Team 1 will try to name three things in response to the cue. They get one point for each correct response. Your instructor will continue to keep score. Choose a different speaker for each cue.

> **EXAMPLE:**
>
> TEAM 2 FIRST SPEAKER: Name three colors that begin with the letter G.
>
> TEAM 1 FIRST SPEAKER: Gray, green, and gold. (3 points)

1. Name three articles of clothing that begin with the letter S.
2. Name three academic subjects that begin with the letter A.
3. Name three composers that begin with the letter B.
4. Name three U.S. states that begin with the letter N.
5. Name three desserts that begin with the letter C.
6. Name three vegetables that begin with the letter P.
7. Name three countries that begin with the letter M.
8. Name three family members that begin with the letter G.

Which team had the highest score? Congratulations!

The Consonants /θ/ and /ð/

| PART ONE | /θ/ and /t/ |

The consonant sound /θ/ (as in the word *thing*) can be at the beginning of a word, in the middle of a word, or at the end of a word.

Beginning	*Middle*	*End*
thumb	no<u>th</u>ing	seven<u>th</u>
thirty	me<u>th</u>od	leng<u>th</u>
theater	ma<u>th</u>ematics	benea<u>th</u>

The consonant sound /t/ (as in the word *time*) can be at the beginning of a word, in the middle of a word, or at the end of a word, too.

Beginning	*Middle*	*End*
teach	six<u>t</u>een	nigh<u>t</u>
Tuesday	ma<u>t</u>erial	upse<u>t</u>
terrible	in<u>t</u>elligent	comple<u>t</u>e

Contrasting the Consonants /θ/ and /t/

 WARM-UP

Look at the pictures. Listen to the words and repeat them.

1. thigh /θ/

2. tie /t/

ARTICULATION

Look at the pictures. The heads show how to make the sounds.

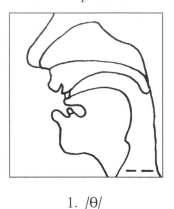

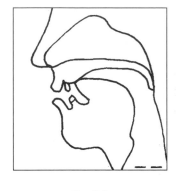

1. /θ/   2. /t/

How are the heads the same? How are the heads different?

CONTRAST

Look at the pairs of words. Listen and repeat.

thank–tank
thought–taught
tenth–tent
eighth–ate

LISTENING

Many words in English have the contrast between /θ/ and /t/. Look again at the *thigh* and *tie* pictures on page 93. /θ/ is *number 1*. /t/ is *number 2*. Listen to the following words. If you hear /θ/ as in thigh, say "one." If you hear /t/ as in tie, say "two."

INTENSIVE PRACTICE

As a class, listen to and repeat the pairs of /θ/ and /t/ words you hear.

PRONOUNCE WORDS

Listen to and repeat the /θ/ words you hear. Then listen to and repeat the /t/ words you hear.

PRONOUNCE PHRASES

Listen to and repeat the phrases you hear.

PRONOUNCE SENTENCES

Listen to and repeat the sentences you hear.

PARTNER 1

1a. LISTENING DISCRIMINATION AND SPEAKING. Pair Practice Words for /θ/ and /t/.   PARTNER 1. Use this page. PARTNER 2. Turn to page 104.

DIRECTIONS: First, you are the speaker. Say the words to your partner. You can see the consonant sound before each word. For example, you say, "Number 1 is *tick*." Repeat any words your partner does not understand.

1.	/t/	tick	5. /t/	mat
2.	/t/	tree	6. /θ/	theme
3.	/θ/	booth	7. /t/	taught
4.	/θ/	threw	8. /θ/	faith

Now you are the listener. Your partner will say some words. Circle the words you hear. Ask your partner to repeat any words you do not understand. Number 9 is an example.

9. (thin) tin		13. thorn torn
10. both boat		14. thank tank
11. thigh tie		15. thigh tie
12. bath bat		16. with wit

Now compare answers with your partner.

PARTNER 1

2a. LISTENING DISCRIMINATION AND SPEAKING. Pair Practice Sentences for /θ/ and /t/.   PARTNER 1. Use this page. PARTNER 2. Turn to page 104.

DIRECTIONS: First, you are the speaker. Say the sentences to your partner. You can see the consonant sound before each sentence. Repeat any sentences your partner does not understand.

1. /t/	Your TEAM is very good.	4. /θ/	I don't believe in FAITH.
2. /θ/	He was a THINKER.	5. /t/	They TAUGHT about the book.
3. /θ/	She left her money in a BOOTH.		

Now you are the listener. Your partner will say some sentences. Circle the word you hear. Ask your partner to repeat any sentences you do not understand. Number 6 is an example.

6. Where's the _____?

   a. thread   b. (tread)

7. She has a _____ voice.

   a. thrilling   b. trilling

8. He wants to take a _____.

   a. bath   b. bat

9. The _____ is green.

   a. three   b. tree

10. The top is _____.

   a. thin   b. tin

Now compare answers with your partner.

3a. ROLE-PLAY. Pair Practice for /θ/ and /t/. PARTNER 1. Use this page. PARTNER 2. Turn to page 105.

DIRECTIONS: Imagine you are a tourist guide. Your partner is a tourist. Your job is tell tourists the location of different hotels, stores, and sites they want to visit. Study the map of Manhattan below. Answer your partner's questions.

EXAMPLE:

TOURIST: Can you please tell me where Tiffany Jewelry is?
GUIDE: Tiffany Jewelry? Of course. It's on Fifth Avenue between 57th Street and 58th Street.
TOURIST: Thank you.

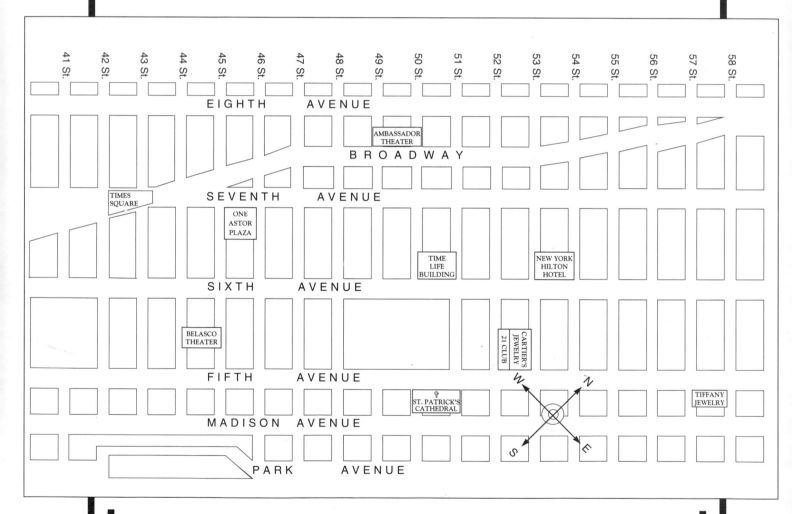

**Challenge! Now tell the tourist how to get from one location to the other in Manhattan.

EXAMPLE:

TOURIST: How do I get from Tiffany Jewelry to Saint Patrick's Cathedral?
GUIDE: Take Fifth Avenue to 51st Street. It's on Fifth Avenue between 50th Street and 51st Street.

/θ/ and /s/

In Part One you saw the sound /θ/ (as in the word _thing_) at the beginning of a word, in the middle of a word, or at the end of a word. The sound /s/ can be at the beginning of a word, in the middle of a word, or at the end of a word, too.

Beginning	_Middle_	_End_
save	passport	face
cereal	December	dress
second	yesterday	price

Contrasting the Consonants /θ/ and /s/

WARM-UP
Look at the pictures. Listen to the words and repeat them.

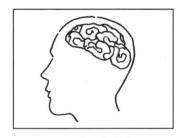

1. think /θ/

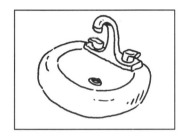

2. sink /s/

ARTICULATION
Look at the pictures. The heads show how to make the sounds.

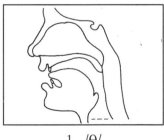

1. /θ/

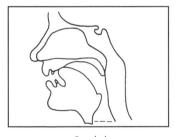

2. /s/

How are the heads the same? How are the heads different?

CONTRAST
Look at the pairs of words. Listen and repeat.
    theme–seem   thick–sick   mouth–mouse   path–pass

LISTENING
Many words in English have the contrast between /θ/ and /s/. Look again at the _think_ and _sink_ pictures above. /θ/ is _number 1_. /s/ is _number 2_. Listen to the following words. If you hear /θ/ as in _think_, say "one." If you hear /s/ as in _sink_, say "two."

INTENSIVE PRACTICE
As a class, listen to and repeat the pairs of /θ/ and /s/ words you hear.

PRONOUNCE WORDS

Listen to and repeat the /θ/ words you hear. Then listen to and repeat the /s/ words you hear.

PRONOUNCE PHRASES

Listen to and repeat the phrases you hear.

PRONOUNCE SENTENCES

Listen to and repeat the sentences you hear.

PRACTICE ACTIVITIES

PARTNER 1

1a. LISTENING DISCRIMINATION AND SPEAKING. Pair Practice Words for /θ/ and /s/. PARTNER 1. Use this page. PARTNER 2. Turn to page 106.

DIRECTIONS: First, you are the speaker. Say the words to your partner. You can see the consonant sound before each word. For example, you say, "Number 1 is *math*." Repeat any words your partner does not understand.

1.	/θ/	math	5. /θ/	thigh
2.	/θ/	growth	6. /θ/	faith
3.	/s/	symbol	7. /θ/	fourth
4.	/s/	sank	8. /s/	worse

Now you are the listener. Your partner will say some words. Circle the words you hear. Ask your partner to repeat any words you do not understand. Number 9 is an example.

9. bath (bass)		13. think	sink
10. thought sought		14. truth	truce
11. thing sing		15. thick	sick
12. tenth tense		16. path	pass

Now compare answers with your partner.

PARTNER 1

2a. LISTENING DISCRIMINATION AND SPEAKING. Pair Practice Sentences for /θ/ and /s/. PARTNER 1. Use this page. PARTNER 2. Turn to page 106.

DIRECTIONS: First, you are the speaker. Say the sentences to your partner. You can see the consonant sound before each sentence. Repeat any sentences your partner does not understand.

1. /θ/ We had THOUGHT it many times.
2. /θ/ He's THAWING the ice.
3. /s/ I admire her FACE.
4. /θ/ How much more is it WORTH?
5. /s/ This one is very SICK.

Now you are the listener. Your partner will say some sentences. Circle the word you hear. Ask your partner to repeat any sentences you do not understand. Number 6 is an example.

6. This _____ is brown.
   a. (moth)   b. moss

7. Put the _____ here.
   a. thimble   b. symbol

8. They argued about the _____.
   a. truth   b. truce

9. She did a good job on my _____.
   a. theme   b. seam

10. Here's a book for _____.
    a. math   b. mass

Now compare answers with your partner.

3a. SPEAKING AND LISTENING. Pair Practice for /θ/ and /s/.   PARTNER 1. Use this page. PARTNER 2. Turn to page 107.

DIRECTIONS: Here is a college schedule with information about classes. You need to know what time and where the classes meet. With your partner, take turns asking and answering questions. Pronounce /θ/ and /s/ correctly. Write the answers on the schedule.

EXAMPLE:

YOU:	When does Ethnography meet?
YOUR PARTNER:	It meets Tuesdays and Thursdays from 10 to 12.
YOU:	Where does it meet?
YOUR PARTNER:	In Thorn Hall room 13.

SCHEDULE OF CLASSES—MATHEWS UNIVERSITY

Class	Day	Time	Room/Building
Anthropology	Mon. Wed.	1–3	10 Thorn Hall
Athletics	_____	_____	_____
Earth Science	Tu. Th.	3–4:30	300 Sullivan
Eastern Thought	_____	_____	_____
18th Century Philosophy	Mon. Tu.	7–10pm	203 Booth Hall
Ethnography	*Tu. Th.*	*10–12*	*13 Thorn Hall*
Health	Mon. Wed.	2–3:30	3 Health Sci.
Mathematics 110	_____	_____	_____
Music Theory	Tu. Th.	7–9pm	113 Simon Hall
Quantum Theory Mechanics	_____	_____	_____
Research Methods	Wed. Fri.	12–2	214 Keith Hall
Theater Arts	_____	_____	_____
Theology	Mon. Wed.	8:30–10	200 Segal Hall
Thermodynamics	_____	_____	_____

Now compare answers with your partner.

4. INTERVIEW AND REPORT. Pair or Small Group Practice for /θ/ and /s/.
DIRECTIONS: Interview a partner or group member about the dates of these American holidays. Write your answers in the blanks. When you are finished, compare your answers with the class. Check a calendar for any answers your class does not know.

    EXAMPLE:
    STUDENT 1: When's St. Patrick's Day?
    STUDENT 2: I think it's the seventeenth of March. When's Washington's Birthday?
    STUDENT 3: I think it's the twentieth of February.
    STUDENT 1: I don't think so. I think it's the twenty-second of February.

HOLIDAYS

Washington's Birthday _____   April Fool's Day _____

Halloween _____   Valentine's Day _____

Independence Day _____   Martin Luther King Jr. Day _____

St. Patrick's Day ___*March 17*___   Flag Day _____

Thanksgiving _____   Lincoln's Birthday _____

PART THREE   **/ð/ and /d/**

The consonant sound /ð/ (as in the word _that_) can be at the beginning of a word or in the middle of a word. Just a few words have /ð/ at the end.

Beginning	*Middle*	*End*
those	either	smooth
there	although	bathe
than	together	breathe

The consonant sound /d/ (as in the word _do_) can be at the beginning of a word, in the middle of a word, or at the end of a word.

Beginning	*Middle*	*End*
deep	Monday	cloud
dollar	reduce	hundred
dangerous	president	understood

Contrasting the Consonants /ð/ and /d/

 WARM-UP
Look at the pictures. Listen to the words and repeat them.

they /ð/   2. day /d/

ARTICULATION
Look at the pictures. The heads show how to make the sounds.

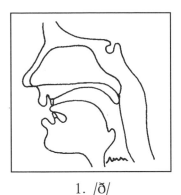

1. /ð/   2. /d/

How are the heads the same? How are the heads different?

CONTRAST
Look at the pairs of words. Listen and repeat.

those–doze

then–den

their–dare

lather–ladder

LISTENING
Some words in English have the contrast between /ð/ and /d/. Look again at the *they* and *day* pictures on page 100. /ð/ is *number 1*. /d/ is *number 2*. Listen to the following words. If you hear /ð/ as in *they*, say "one." If you hear /d/ as in *day*, say "two."

INTENSIVE PRACTICE
As a class, listen to and repeat the pairs of /ð/ and /d/ words you hear.

PRONOUNCE WORDS
Listen to and repeat the /ð/ words you hear. Then listen to and repeat the /d/ words you hear.

PRONOUNCE PHRASES
Listen to and repeat the phrases you hear.

PRONOUNCE SENTENCES
Listen to and repeat the sentences you hear.

PARTNER 1

1a. LISTENING DISCRIMINATION AND SPEAKING. Pair Practice Words for /ð/ and /d/.   PARTNER 1. Use this page. PARTNER 2. Turn to page 108.

DIRECTIONS: First, you are the speaker. Say the words to your partner. You can see the consonant sound before each word. For example, you say, "Number 1 is *though.*" Repeat any words your partner does not understand.

1. /ð/   though
2. /d/   Dan
3. /ð/   loathing
4. /d/   day
5. /ð/   worthy
6. /ð/   then

Now you are the listener. Your partner will say some words. Circle the words you hear. Ask your partner to repeat any words you do not understand. Number 7 is an example.

7. (those)   doze
8. lather   ladder
9. soothe   sued
10. then   den
11. breathing   breeding
12. there   dare

Now compare answers with your partner.

PARTNER 1

2a. LISTENING DISCRIMINATION AND SPEAKING. Pair Practice Sentences for /ð/ and /d/.   PARTNER 1. Use this page. PARTNER 2. Turn to page 108.

DIRECTIONS: First, you are the speaker. Say the sentences to your partner. You can see the consonant sound before each sentence. Repeat any sentences your partner does not understand.

1. /ð/   THEY'VE called you.
2. /ð/   Is THIS RESPECT what you wanted?
3. /d/   The LADDER isn't good.
4. /d/   Can you spell "DOUGH"?

Now you are the listener. Your partner will say some sentences. Circle the word you hear. Ask your partner to repeat any sentences you do not understand. Number 5 is an example.

5. _____ will come soon.
    a. They   b. (Day)
6. Can it _____?
    a. breathe   b. breed
7. His contract is _____.
    a. worthy   b. wordy
8. They _____ her.
    a. soothe   b. sued

Now compare answers with your partner.

3. SPEAKING. Creative Connections. Small Group Game to Practice /ð/ and /d/.

DIRECTIONS: You and your group need to use the short sentences and connecting words to create longer sentences. When you are finished, tell your sentences to the whole class.

> **EXAMPLE:**
> They had decided to go on a diet. (even though)
> Even though they had decided to go on a diet, they ordered dessert.
>
> OR
>
> They had decided to go on a diet even though they weren't overweight.

1. They studied the diagram. (nevertheless)
2. The building was a long distance away. (although)
3. The audience was bored. (on the other hand)
4. The doctor made another appointment. (even though)
5. They gathered the data themselves. (on the other hand)
6. Her father is late for the wedding. (although)
7. The weather is windy and cold. (furthermore)   *next.*
8. She'd rather not use a dictionary. (even though)

Which group made the most creative sentences? Congratulations!

4. REPORT. Cities and Countries.

DIRECTIONS: Compare two cities or two countries that you have lived in. Use the verbs and words below to make your comparisons.

> **EXAMPLE:**
> New York City is more crowded than Tehran, but Tehran has better weather than New York City.

WORD LISTS

verb: *to be*	verb: *to have*
dirty	good weather
crowded	old buildings
windy	diverse neighborhoods
cold	big downtown
dangerous	pedestrians
wonderful	industrial districts
modern	shopping districts

1b. LISTENING DISCRIMINATION AND SPEAKING. Pair Practice Words for /θ/ and /t/. PARTNER 2. Use this page. PARTNER 1. Turn to page 95.

DIRECTIONS: First, you are the listener. Your partner will say some words. Circle the words you hear. Ask your partner to repeat any words you do not understand. Number 1 is an example.

1. thick   (tick)
2. three   tree
3. booth   boot
4. threw   true

5. math   mat
6. theme   team
7. thought   taught
8. faith   fate

Now you are the speaker. Say the words to your partner. You can see the consonant sound before each word. For example, you say, "Number 9 is *thin*." Repeat any words your partner does not understand.

9. /θ/   thin
10. /t/   boat
11. /θ/   thigh
12. /θ/   bath

13. /t/   torn
14. /θ/   thank
15. /θ/   thigh
16. /t/   wit

Now compare answers with your partner.

2b. LISTENING DISCRIMINATION AND SPEAKING. Pair Practice Sentences for /θ/ and /t/. PARTNER 2. Use this page. PARTNER 1. Turn to page 95.

DIRECTIONS: First, you are the listener. Your partner will say some sentences. Circle the word you hear. Ask your partner to repeat any sentences you do not understand. Number 1 is an example.

1. Your _____ is very good.
   a. theme   b. (team)

2. He was a _____.
   a. thinker   b. tinker

3. She left her money in a _____.
   a. booth   b. boot

4. I don't believe in _____.
   a. faith   b. fate

5. They _____ about the book.
   a. thought   b. taught

Now you are the speaker. Say the sentences to your partner. You can see the consonant sound before each sentence. Repeat any sentences your partner does not understand.

6. /t/   Where's the TREAD?
7. /θ/   She has a THRILLING voice.
8. /t/   He wants to take a BAT.
9. /θ/   The THREE is green.
10. /θ/   The top is THIN.

Now compare answers with your partner.

PAIR PRACTICE: Partner 2

3b. ROLE-PLAY. PAIR PRACTICE FOR /θ/ AND /t/. PARTNER 2. Use this page.

PARTNER 1. Turn to page 96.

DIRECTIONS: Imagine you are a tourist. Your partner is a tourist guide. You want to visit the stores and sites numbered on the list. Ask the tourist guide where these places are. Mark their numbers on the map of Manhattan.

EXAMPLE:

TOURIST: Can you please tell me where Tiffany Jewelry is?

GUIDE: Tiffany Jewelry? Of course. It's on Fifth Avenue between 57th Street and 58th Street.

TOURIST: Thank you.

SITES

1. Times Square
2. Twenty-One Club
3. Belasco Theater
4. N.Y. Hilton Hotel
5. Tiffany Jewelry

6. One Astor Plaza
7. Cartier's Jewelry
8. Time Life Building
9. St. Patrick's Cathedral
10. Ambassador Theater

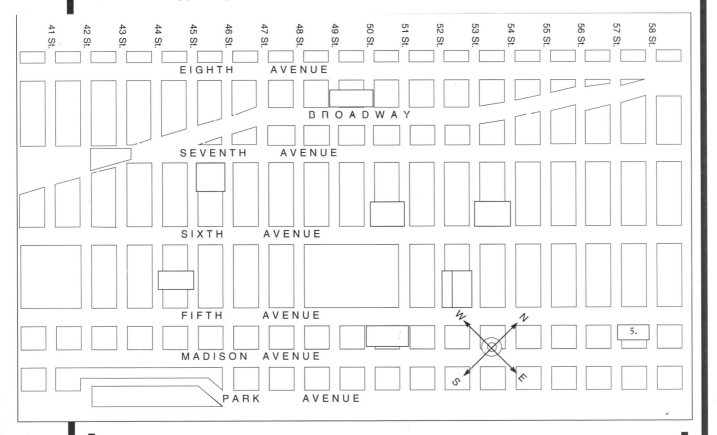

**Challenge! Now ask the tourist guide how to get from one location to the other in Manhattan.

EXAMPLE:

TOURIST: How do I get from Tiffany Jewelry to Saint Patrick's Cathedral?

GUIDE: Take Fifth Avenue to 51st Street. It's on Fifth Avenue between 50th Street and 51st Street.

1b. LISTENING DISCRIMINATION AND SPEAKING. Pair Practice Words for /θ/ and /s/. PARTNER 2. Use this page. PARTNER 1. Turn to page 98.

DIRECTIONS: First, you are the listener. Your partner will say some words. Circle the words you hear. Ask your partner to repeat any words you do not understand. Number 1 is an example.

1. (math)   mass
2. growth   gross
3. thimble   symbol
4. thank   sank

5. thigh   sigh
6. faith   face
7. fourth   force
8. worth   worse

Now you are the speaker. Say the words to your partner. You can see the consonant sound before each word. For example, you say, "Number 9 is *bass*." Repeat any words your partner does not understand.

9. /s/   bass
10. /θ/ thought
11. /s/ sing
12. /θ/ tenth

13. /s/ sink
14. /s/ truce
15. /θ/ thick
16. /θ/ path

Now compare answers with your partner.

2b. LISTENING DISCRIMINATION AND SPEAKING. Pair Practice Sentences for /θ/ and /s/. PARTNER 2. Use this page. PARTNER 1. Turn to page 98.

DIRECTIONS: First, you are the listener. Your partner will say some sentences. Circle the word you hear. Ask your partner to repeat any sentences you do not understand. Number 1 is an example.

1. We had _____ it many times.
   a. (thought)   b. sought
2. He's _____ the ice.
   a. thawing   b. sawing
3. I admire her _____.
   a. faith   b. face

4. How much more is it _____?
   a. worth   b. worse
5. This one is very _____.
   a. thick   b. sick

Now you are the speaker. Say the sentences to your partner. You can see the consonant sound before each sentence. Repeat any sentences your partner does not understand.

6. /θ/   This MOTH is brown.
7. /s/   Put the SYMBOL here.
8. /s/   They argued about the TRUCE.
9. /θ/   She did a good job on my THEME.
10. /θ/ Here's a book for MATH.

Now compare answers with your partner.

PAIR PRACTICE: Partner 2

3b. SPEAKING AND LISTENING. Pair Practice for /θ/ and /s/.

PARTNER 2. Use this page. PARTNER 1. Turn to page 99.

DIRECTIONS: Here is a college schedule with information about classes. You need to know what time and where the classes meet. With your partner, take turns asking and answering questions. Pronounce /θ/ and /s/ correctly. Write the answers on the schedule.

EXAMPLE:

YOU:	When does Research Methods meet?
YOUR PARTNER:	It meets Wednesdays and Fridays from 12 to 2.
YOU:	Where does it meet?
YOUR PARTNER:	In Keith Hall room 214.

SCHEDULE OF CLASSES—MATHEWS UNIVERSITY

Class	Day	Time	Room/Building
Anthropology	_____	_____	_____
Athletics	Daily	8–9	303 Gym
Earth Science	_____	_____	_____
Eastern Thought	Wed. Fri.	5–6:30 PM	113 Booth Hall
18th Century Philosophy	_____	_____	_____
Ethnography	Tu. Th.	10–12	13 Thorn Hall
Health	_____	_____	_____
Mathematics 110	Mon. Wed.	7–10 PM	203 Sullivan
Music Theory	_____	_____	_____
Quantum Theory Mechanics	M.Tu.W.Th.	9–10	400 South Hall
Research Methods	*Wed. Fri.*	*12–2*	*214 Keith Hall*
Theater Arts	Wed. Thu.	1–3	10 Grand Theater
Theology	_____	_____	_____
Thermodynamics	Tu. Th.	9:30–11	330 South Hall

Now compare answers with your partner

1b. LISTENING DISCRIMINATION AND SPEAKING. Pair Practice Words for /ð/ and /d/. PARTNER 2. Use this page. PARTNER 1. Turn to page 102.

DIRECTIONS: First, you are the listener. Your partner will say some words. Circle the words you hear. Ask your partner to repeat any words you do not understand. Number 1 is an example.

1. (though) dough   4. they   day
2. than   Dan   5. worthy wordy
3. loathing loading   6. then   den

Now you are the speaker. Say the words to your partner. You can see the consonant sound before each word. For example, you say, "Number 7 is *those*." Repeat any words your partner does not understand.

7. /ð/ those   10. /ð/ then
8. /d/ ladder   11. /d/ breeding
9. /ð/ soothe   12. /d/ dare

Now compare answers with your partner.

2b. LISTENING DISCRIMINATION AND SPEAKING. Pair Practice Sentences for /ð/ and /d/. PARTNER 2. Use this page. PARTNER 1. Turn to page 102.

DIRECTIONS: First, you are the listener. Your partner will say some sentences. Circle the word you hear. Ask your partner to repeat any sentences you do not understand. Number 1 is an example.

1. _____ called you.   3. The _____ isn't good.

   a. (They've)   b. Dave   a. lather   b. ladder

2. Is _____ what you wanted?   4. Can you spell _____?

   a. this respect   b. disrespect   a. "though"   b. "dough"

Now you are the speaker. Say the sentences to your partner. You can see the consonant sound before each sentence. Repeat any sentences your partner does not understand.

5. /d/ DAY will come soon.
6. /ð/ Can it BREATHE?
7. /ð/ His contract is WORTHY.
8. /d/ They SUED her.

Now compare answers with your partner.

PAIR PRACTICE: Partner 2

The Consonants /l/ and /r/

In English, the consonant sound /l/ can appear at the beginning of a word, in the middle of a word, or at the end of a word.

Beginning	Middle	End
light	se*l*dom	spe*ll*
listen	po*l*ite	peop*l*e
language	use*l*ess	beautifu*l*

The consonant sound /r/ can also appear at the beginning of a word, in the middle of a word, or at the end of a word.

Beginning	Middle	End
round	ma*r*ket	wea*r*
raise	ca*rr*y	unde*r*
reason	pa*r*don	neighbo*r*

Contrasting the Consonants /l/ and /r/

 WARM-UP

Look at the pictures. Listen to the words and repeat them.

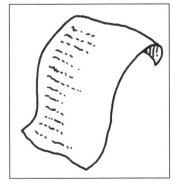

1. list /l/

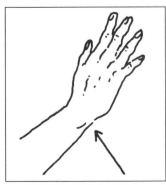

2. wrist /r/

ARTICULATION

Look at the pictures. The heads show how to make the sounds.

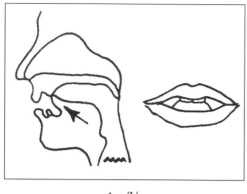

1. /l/   2. /r/

How are the heads the same? How are the heads and lips different?

CONTRAST

Look at the pairs of words. Listen and repeat.

low–row   lamp–ramp
lock–rock   lead–read

LISTENING

Many words in English have the contrast between /l/ and /r/. Look again at the *list* and *wrist* pictures on page 109. /l/ is *number 1*. /r/ is *number 2*. Listen to the following words. If you hear /l/ as in *list*, say "one." If you hear /r/ as in *wrist*, say "two."

INTENSIVE PRACTICE

As a class, listen to and repeat the pairs of /l/ and /r/ words you hear.

PRONOUNCE WORDS

Listen to and repeat the /l/ words you hear. Then listen to and repeat the /r/ words you hear.

/l/ AND /r/ AFTER VOWELS

Say the vowel /ə/ *before* /l/ or /r/ to clearly pronounce /l/ or /r/. Your tongue relaxes and becomes flat when you say /ə/. Then shape your tongue forward for /l/ or curl it backward for /r/.

Listen to these examples:

/diy/, /əl/, /diyəl/ (deal)
/diy/, /ər/, /diyər/ (dear)

Now listen to and repeat the pairs of sounds and words with /l/ and /r/ after vowels.

/fiy/, /əl/, /fiyəl/ (feel)   /fiy/, /ər/, /fiyər/ (fear)
/wiy/, /əl/, /wiyəl/ (we'll)   /wiy/, /ər/, /wiyər/ (we're)
/fey/, /əl/, /feyəl/ (fail)   /fey/, /ər/, /feyər/ (fair)
/taw/, /əl/, /tawəl/ (towel)   /taw/, /ər/, /tawər/ (tower)

Look at the pictures. Listen to the words and repeat them.

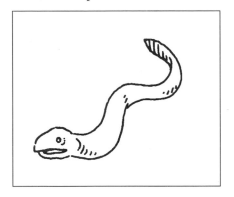 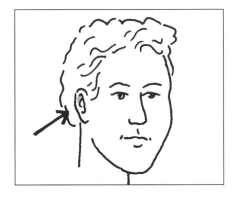

1. eel /l/   2. ear /r/

🔊 **CONTRAST**

Look at the pairs of words. Listen and repeat.

call–car

kneel–near

pole–pour

tile–tire

🔊 **LISTENING**

Some words in English have the contrast between /l/ and /r/ after vowels. Look again at the *eel* and *ear* pictures above. /l/ is *number 1*. /r/ is *number 2*. Listen to the following words. If you hear /l/ at the end as in *eel*, say "one." If you hear /r/ at the end as in *ear*, say "two."

🔊 **INTENSIVE PRACTICE**

As a class, listen to and repeat the pairs of /l/ and /r/ words you hear.

🔊 **PRONOUNCE WORDS**

Listen to and repeat the /l/ words you hear. Then listen to and repeat the /r/ words you hear.

🔊 **PRONOUNCE PHRASES**

Listen to and repeat the phrases you hear.

🔊 **PRONOUNCE SENTENCES**

Listen to and repeat the sentences you hear.

PARTNER 1

1a. LISTENING DISCRIMINATION AND SPEAKING. Pair Practice Words for /l/ and /r/. PARTNER 1. Use this page. PARTNER 2. Turn to page 115.

DIRECTIONS: First, you are the speaker. Say the words to your partner. The consonant sound you should pronounce is before each word. For example, you say "Number 1 is *lime.*" Repeat any words your partner does not understand.

1. /l/ lime	3. /r/ wrap	5. /r/ ride	7. /r/ correct
2. /l/ older	4. /l/ late	6. /r/ write	8. /l/ ball

Now you are the listener. Your partner will say some words. Circle the words you hear. Ask your partner to repeat any words you do not understand. Number 9 is an example.

9. (lot) rot	11. fall far	13. heel hear	15. pail pair
10. alive arrive	12. lies rise	14. loyal lawyer	16. lake rake

Now compare answers with your partner.

PARTNER 1

2a. LISTENING DISCRIMINATION AND SPEAKING. Pair Practice Sentences for /l/ and /r/. PARTNER 1. Use this page. PARTNER 2. Turn to page 115.

DIRECTIONS: First, you are the speaker. Say the sentences to your partner. The consonant sound you should pronounce is before each sentence. Repeat any sentences your partner does not understand.

1. /r/ Your answer is WRONG.
2. /l/ How many did you COLLECT?
3. /r/ You can't STEER a car.
4. /l/ I want the LIGHT one.
5. /r/ A RAM is a kind of sheep.

Now you are the listener. Your partner will say some sentences. Circle the word you hear. Ask your partner to repeat any sentences you do not understand. Number 6 is an example.

6. We can't use this _____.
   a. (tile)   b. tire
7. Do you see the _____ ?
   a. lamp   b. ramp
8. It's a book about a _____.
   a. pilot   b. pirate
9. The game is _____.
   a. bowling   b. boring
10. It was lost in the _____.
   a. file   b. fire

Now compare answers with your partner.

3. SPEAKING. Symbols. Pair Practice for /l/ and /r/.

DIRECTIONS: How well do you and your partner know these symbols? Take turns asking and answering questions. Pronounce /l/ and /r/ correctly.

EXAMPLE:
STUDENT 1:   What's the meaning of symbol number 8?
STUDENT 2:   Approximately. What's the meaning of symbol number...?

1. +
2. =
3. >
4. <
5. ≠
6. √

7. °
8. ≈
9. %
10. #
11. $
12. ©

PARTNER 1

4a. SPEAKING AND LISTENING. Pair Practice for /l/ and /r/.
PARTNER 1. Use this page. PARTNER 2. Turn to page 116.

DIRECTIONS: Imagine you and your partner are doing a survey on students' musical tastes. You each already have some information. Take turns asking and answering questions to complete your survey. Pronounce /l/ and /r/ correctly.

EXAMPLE:
YOU: How often does Ray listen to rhythm and blues music?
YOUR PARTNER: Sometimes. How often does Rebecca listen to classical music?
YOU: Rarely. How often does . . .

SURVEY ON STUDENTS' MUSIC TASTES

	Carol	Larry	Doris	Ray	Barbara	Robert	Rebecca	Lou
religious		x		xxx		xx	x	
classical	xxx		xxx				x	
rhythm & blues	x	xx		xx	xxx		xxx	
rock			x			xxx		x
country & western	xx	x		xxx	xx		x	
rap		xx		x		xx	xxx	
reggae	xxx		xx	x		xxx		x
latin		xxx	xx		x		xx	
jazz			xxx	xx		x		x

xxx = almost always   **xx = sometimes**   **x = rarely**

5. ROLE-PLAY. Vacation Tours. Group Practice for /l/ and /r/.

DIRECTIONS: Here is a travel booklet. One student is the travel agent and the others are customers. Take turns being the agent and a customer. The customers need to ask about places they want to visit. Use information in the booklet to ask and answer questions.

EXAMPLE:

TRAVEL AGENT: May I help you?
CUSTOMER 1:   Yes. We'd like information about a tour to Africa.
TRAVEL AGENT: We have some tours to Africa. They go to Liberia, Morocco, and Ivory Coast.
CUSTOMER 2:   When's the tour to Morocco?
TRAVEL AGENT: It leaves July 1 and returns July 21.
CUSTOMER 1:   How much does it cost?
TRAVEL AGENT: $832.
CUSTOMER 2:   Sounds great! We'll take it.

ISLAND CRUISES
• Blue water, white beaches of...
GREECE
— $999 —
July 1–July 22
U.S.S. Regal

• Exotic sites, duty-free gems...
U.S. VIRGIN ISLANDS
10 days of heaven for **$660**
June 28–July 7

• Cruise to,,,
PUERTO RICO
Direct from Miami
April 10–May 5
U.S.S. Starline
$820

MIDDLE EAST
• Exotic, historic...
ISRAEL
$795
2 weeks
Non-stop direct from NY
June 5–June 19
Air Israel & World Class Hotel

EUROPE
• Fine food and wines...
PARIS, FRANCE
Air France & Grand Hotel
July 4–July 25 — Special! **$999**

• There's nothing like...
GERMANY
Berlin – Munich
June 20–June 30
Rail Pass + Day Tours
$600

• Visit historic,,,
ROME, ITALY
NY → Rome → NY
July 15–August 3
$899 4-Star Hotel

SOUTH AMERICA
• Beaches, carnivals...
BRAZIL
Latin Air to Rio
April 8–April 30
$850

• You'll never forget...
HONDURAS
Markets, Tours, More!
June 1–17, only **$649**

ASIA
• Unforgettable sites of ...
SEOUL, KOREA
Non-stop Korean Air
Far East Hotel
July 15–August 2
$999

• The best of the Far East
is in...
MYANMAR (BURMA)
March 15–April 3
Special Spring Tour Price
$649

• Smiling faces await you in,,,
SINGAPORE
Two weeks
Too good to be true!
July 5–July 19
Rising Sun Hotel
Only **$899**

AFRICA
• Sun and fun in ...
LIBERIA
Markets, Music, More!
AirAfrica—20 days
$1,150
May 29–June 17
World Class Hotel

• Visit the beautiful beaches of...
MOROCCO
Day Tours, Shopping
Direct from L.A.
July 1–July 21
American Air Non-stop
Only **$832**

• Get away from it all,,,
IVORY COAST
Exotic and warm
$600
(Spring Tour)
March 15–April 1
Golden Hotel Suite

---

6. INTERVIEW AND REPORT. Group Survey on Favorite Music. Group Activity to Practice /l/ and /r/.

DIRECTIONS: You and your group can use the types of music in **Activity 4** to ask each other questions about what each of you listens to. Then different members of your group can report to the class on:

a.   What types of music none of you listens to.
b.   What types of music only one person in your group listens to.
c.   Who listens to the most different types of music.
d.   What types of music are most popular among all of you.
e.   What types of music your group would like to know more about.

1b. LISTENING DISCRIMINATION AND SPEAKING. Pair Practice Words for /l/ and /r/. PARTNER 2. Use this page. PARTNER 1. Turn to page 112.

DIRECTIONS: First, you are the listener. Your partner will say some words. Circle the words you hear. Ask your partner to repeat any words you do not understand. Number 1 is an example.

1. (lime) rhyme	3. lap wrap	5. lied ride	7. collect correct
2. older order	4. late rate	6. light write	8. ball bar

Now you are the speaker. Say the words to your partner. The consonant sound you should pronounce is before each word. For example, you say "Number 9 is lot." Repeat any words your partner does not understand.

9. /l/ lot	11. /l/ fall	13. /l/ heel	15. /r/ pair
10. /r/ arrive	12. /r/ rise	14. /l/ loyal	16. /r/ rake

Now compare answers with your partner.

2b. LISTENING DISCRIMINATION AND SPEAKING. Pair Practice Sentences for /l/ and /r/. PARTNER 2. Use this page. PARTNER 1. Turn to page 112.

DIRECTIONS: First, you are the listener. Your partner will say some sentences. Circle the word you hear. Ask your partner to repeat any sentences you do not understand. Number 1 is an example.

1. Your answer is _____.
   a. long   b. (wrong)
2. How many did you _____?
   a. collect   b. correct
3. You can't _____ a car.
   a. steal   b. steer
4. I want the _____ one.
   a. light   b. right
5. A _____ is a kind of sheep.
   a. lamb   b. ram

Now you are the speaker. Say the sentences to your partner. The consonant sound you should pronounce is before each sentence. Repeat any sentences your partner does not understand.

6. /l/ We can't use this TILE.
7. /r/ Do you see the RAMP?
8. /l/ It's a book about a PILOT.
9. /l/ The game is BOWLING.
10. /r/ It was lost in the FIRE.

Now compare answers with your partner.

4b. SPEAKING AND LISTENING. Pair Practice for /l/ and /r/.

PARTNER 2. Use this page. PARTNER 1. Turn to page 113.

DIRECTIONS: Imagine you and your partner are doing a survey on students' musical tastes. You each already have some information. Take turns asking and answering questions to complete your survey. Pronounce /l/ and /r/ correctly.

EXAMPLE:

YOU:	How often does Rebecca listen to classical music?
YOUR PARTNER:	Rarely. How often does Ray listen to rhythm and blues music?
YOU:	Sometimes. How often does . . .

- -

SURVEY ON STUDENTS' MUSIC TASTES

	Carol	Larry	Doris	Ray	Barbara	Robert	Rebecca	Lou
religious	xx		xxx		x			xx
classical		xx		x	xxx	xx	x	xx
rhythm & blues			xxx	xx		x		xx
rock	xx	xxx		x	xx		xx	
country & western			x			xxx		xxx
rap	xxx		x		xxx			x
reggae		xx			x		xx	
latin	x			x		xx		xxx
jazz	x	xxx			x		xxx	

xxx = almost always   xx = sometimes   x = rarely

Consonants at the Beginning and End of Words

Stop Consonants at the Beginning and End of Words

Some consonants in English are made when air is stopped for a very short time with the lips or tongue. They are called *stop consonants*.

FIGURE IT OUT

What two consonants are made by stopping the air with two lips? Write them here: /p/, /b/

What two consonants are made by stopping the air with the tongue on the tooth ridge? Write them here: /t/, /d/

What two consonants are made by stopping the air with the back of the tongue on the top of the mouth? Write them here: /k/, /g/

COMPARING STOP CONSONANTS AT THE BEGINNING OF WORDS

Listen to these pairs of words:

pie	buy	tip	dip
pest	best	could	good
toe	dough	curl	girl

To clearly pronounce stop consonants at the beginning of words, push the air from your lips when you say /p/, /t/, or /k/. Put your hand in front of your mouth. Say /p/, /t/, /k/. You can feel the air. Do not push the air from your lips when you say /b/, /d/, or /g/.

Listen to the pairs of words again and repeat them.

Now say these pairs of words with stop consonants at the beginning. Push the air from your lips when you say /p/, /t/, or /k/.

pack	back	tie	die
pig	big	cane	gain
two	do	cot	got

COMPARING STOP CONSONANTS AT THE END OF WORDS

Listen to these pairs of words:

mop	mob		hit	hid
cap	cab		duck	dug
neat	need		back	bag

To clearly pronounce stop consonants at the end of words, say the vowel before /b/, /d/, and /g/ long. Say the vowel before /p/, /t/, and /k/ short. Do not push air from your lips for /p/, /t/, and /k/ at the end of words.

All stop consonants at the end of words are quiet. To make them quiet, stop the consonant and do not open your lips or tongue again.

Listen to the pairs of words again and repeat them.

Now say these pairs of words with stop consonants at the end. Say the vowel before /b/, /d/, or /g/ long. Stop the consonants at the end, and do not open your lips or tongue again.

EXAMPLE:

hit   hi:d

short vowel   *long vowel*

lap	la:b
rope	ro:be
not	no:d
set	sai:d
tack	ta:g
pick	pi:g

INTENSIVE PRACTICE

As a class, listen to and repeat the pairs of words you hear.

PRACTICE ACTIVITIES

1. LISTENING DISCRIMINATION.

DIRECTIONS: You see some pairs of words. You will hear only one word. Circle the word you hear.

EXAMPLES:

(pest)   best

neat   (need)

1. path   bath
2. tear   dear
3. card   guard
4. town   down
5. came   game
6. rip   rib
7. light   lied
8. seat   seed

2a. LISTENING DISCRIMINATION AND SPEAKING. Pair Practice Words for Stop Consonants. PARTNER 1. Use this page. PARTNER 2. Turn to page 125.

DIRECTIONS: First, you are the speaker. Say the words to your partner. For example, you say, "Number 1 is *peach*." Repeat any words your partner does not understand.

1. peach
2. dime
3. gave
4. base
5. ton

6. come
7. cup
8. led
9. sag
10. kit

Now you are the listener. Your partner will say some words. Circle the words you hear. Ask your partner to repeat any words you do not understand. Number 11 is an example.

11. pear (bear)
12. touch Dutch
13. coat goat
14. pay bay
15. ten den

16. coal goal
17. nap nab
18. hat had
19. clock clog
20. feet feed

Now compare answers with your partner.

3a. LISTENING DISCRIMINATION AND SPEAKING. Pair Practice Sentences for Stop Consonants. PARTNER 1. Use this page. PARTNER 2. Turn to page 125.

DIRECTIONS: First, you are the speaker. Say the sentences to your partner. Repeat any sentences your partner does not understand.

1. We saw a PAIR at the zoo.
2. He seems kind of TENSE.
3. Joe is the man in the CAB.

4. I bought a WHITE belt.
5. There's a SNAG in my pocket.

Now you are the listener. Your partner will say some sentences. Circle the word you hear. Ask your partner to repeat any sentences you do not understand. Number 6 is an example.

6. You need a _____ to finish this job.
   a. (push)   b. bush

7. Do you have the _____ ?
   a. time   b. dime

8. Where is my _____ ?
   a. rope   b. robe

9. Here's a _____ for you.
   a. seat   b. seed

10. Don't step on that _____ .
    a. tack   b. tag

Now compare answers with your partner.

4a. SPEAKING AND LISTENING. Pair Practice for Stop Consonants.

PARTNER 1. Use this page. PARTNER 2. Turn to page 126.

DIRECTIONS: Here are some abbreviations. Ask your partner what they mean. Write the meanings next to the abbreviations.

EXAMPLE:

YOU: What does PA mean?
YOUR PARTNER: It means "Pennsylvania."

PA *Pennsylvania*

1. P.O.B. _____

2. Ph.D. _____

3. Blvd. _____

4. AK _____

5. kg. _____

Now your partner will ask you about these abbreviations. Listen carefully because the abbreviations are not in the same order as the questions. Repeat any answers your partner does not understand.

EXAMPLE:

YOUR PARTNER: What does PL mean?
YOU: It means "Place."

ABBREVIATIONS

dept. = department
KS = Kansas
pt.= pint
Sept. = September
Tpke. = Turnpike

5. REPORT. Hot Topic. Class Activity to Practice Stop Consonants.

DIRECTIONS: What are the people in your country or city concerned about? Choose one "hot" topic from the list. Tell the class about people's hopes, opinions, or fears.

1. world peace
2. terrorism
3. urban development
4. employment conditions
5. pollution
6. domestic economy
7. population control
8. public health care
9. nuclear power
10. politics

-s and -ed Endings

Pronunciation of -s and -ed endings in English is important. English speakers use these endings very often, and they have several different grammatical meanings.

EXAMPLES:

-s

Plane<u>s</u> are faster than train<u>s</u>. (plural nouns)

This is the advisor'<u>s</u> office. (possessive)

Joe work<u>s</u> every weekend. (third person singular verb)

She'<u>s</u> taking a test. (contraction for "is")

It'<u>s</u> been a cold winter. (contraction for "has")

-ed

They visit<u>ed</u> a museum. (past tense verb)

Here's the revis<u>ed</u> report. (adjective)

I've own<u>ed</u> my car a year.

The movie had end<u>ed</u> early.   }   (past participles)

The check was just cash<u>ed</u>.   }

FIGURE IT OUT

In English, the pronunciation of -s endings is regular. -s can sound like /z/, /s/, or like a separate syllable /ɪz/. Listen to these examples of words with -s endings.

Words ending in voiceless sounds:		*Words ending in voiced sounds:*		*Words ending in noisy consonants:*	
ending sound	word	ending sound	word	ending sound	word
/p/	kee<u>ps</u>	/b/	ca<u>bs</u>	/s/	dre<u>sses</u>
/t/	wai<u>ts</u>	/d/	gra<u>des</u>	/z/	clo<u>ses</u>
/k/	boo<u>ks</u>	/g/	dra<u>gs</u>	/ʃ/	wi<u>shes</u>
/f/	lau<u>ghs</u>	/v/	gi<u>ves</u>	/tʃ/	ma<u>tches</u>
/θ/	ear<u>th's</u>	/ð/	brea<u>thes</u>	/dʒ/	a<u>ges</u>
		/m/	roo<u>ms</u>		
		/n/	pla<u>ns</u>		
		/ŋ/	si<u>ngs</u>		
		/l/	trave<u>ls</u>		
		/r/	sto<u>res</u>		
		vowel sounds {	go<u>es</u> he'<u>s</u> da<u>ys</u>		

Which sound do you hear for -s in each group of words: /z/, /s/, or /ɪz/? Write some rules.

RULES FOR -S ENDINGS:

1. When a word ends in a voiceless sound, add -s and pronounce -s like /   /.

2. When a word ends in a voiced sound, add -s and pronounce -s like /   /.

3. When a word ends in a noisy consonant, add -s and pronounce -s like /   /.

The pronunciation of -ed endings is regular, too. -ed can sound like /d/, like /t/, or like a separate syllable /ɪd/. Listen to these examples of words with -ed endings.

Words ending in voiceless sounds:		Words ending in voiced sounds:		Words ending in /t/ or /d/:	
ending sound	word	ending sound	word	ending sound	word
/p/	stopped	/b/	robbed	/t/	cheated
/k/	talked	/g/	jogged		painted
/f/	knifed	/v/	loved		started
/s/	placed	/ð/	breathed	/d/	needed
/ʃ/	pushed	/z/	raised		guided
/tʃ/	reached	/dʒ/	changed		included
		/m/	dreamed		
		/n/	learned		
		/ŋ/	wronged		
		/l/	called		
		/r/	answered		
		vowel sounds {	showed / cried / stayed		

Which sound do you hear for -ed in each group of words: /d/, /t/, or /ɪd/? Write some rules.

RULES FOR -ED ENDINGS

1. When a word ends in a voiceless sound, add -ed and pronounce -ed like / /.

2. When a word ends in a voiced sound, add -ed and pronounce -ed like / /.

3. When a word ends in /t/ or /d/, add -ed and pronounce -ed like / /.

PRONOUNCE -S AND -ED ENDINGS.

Listen to the words with -s and -ed endings on pages 121 and 122 and repeat them. Then say them on your own. Read one word from each column, going across. Pronounce -s and -ed correctly.

EXAMPLES:

keeps	cabs	dresses
/s/	/z/	/ɪz/
stopped	robbed	cheated
/t/	/d/	/ɪd/

PRACTICE ACTIVITIES

1. SPEAKING. Small Group Practice for -ed.

Here are two pictures of the Wilsons' house. **A** is the house two years ago when they bought it. **B** is their house today after they had it remodeled.

DIRECTIONS: Take turns with other students in your group. Make sentences about what the Wilsons had done to their house. Pronounce -ed on past participles correctly.

EXAMPLE:

STUDENT 1:   They had the shutters remov<u>ed</u>.
STUDENT 2:   They had the swimming pool install<u>ed</u>.
STUDENT 3:   They had some new trees plant<u>ed</u>.

PARTNER 1

2a. LISTENING DISCRIMINATION AND SPEAKING. Pair Practice for -s.
PARTNER 1. Use this page. PARTNER 2. Turn to page 126.

DIRECTIONS: First ask your partner the questions. For example, you say, "What make<u>s</u> you *sad?*"
Listen to and correct your partner for *-s* on verbs and nouns.

1.   What makes you sad?   4.   . . . laugh?
2.   . . . afraid?   5.   . . . proud?
3.   . . . tired?   6.   . . . uncomfortable?

Now listen to your partner's questions and answer them. Pronounce *-s* on plural nouns or on
the verb in your answers.

     EXAMPLE:

     YOUR PARTNER: What makes you angry?
     YOU: Pop quizz<u>es</u> make me angry.   OR   A bad grade make<u>s</u> me angry.

3. INTERVIEW. Pair Practice for *-s* and *-ed.*

DIRECTIONS: Interview a partner. Use the cues to ask questions. You can take notes to help you remember your partner's answers.

EXAMPLES:
(cue) . . . live in this city?
YOU: How long have you liv<u>ed</u> in this city?

Your partner will interview you, too. Choose who will ask or answer first. After the interviews, tell the class about your partner. You can use your notes. When you speak to the class about your partner, say "she" or "he" and use *-s* as a contraction for has. Pronounce *-ed* endings on past participles, too.

CUES

1. . . . live in this city?
2. . . . live in your present apartment or house?
3. . . . work at your present job?
4. . . . study English at this school?
5. . . . need to improve your English?
6. . . . enjoy speaking English?
7. . . . use this book to practice?
8. . . . own an English dictionary?

4. DISCUSS AND REPORT. Small Group Practice for *-s.*

DIRECTIONS: Here are a list of gifts and a list of people.

Discuss with your group which gift is most appropriate for each person listed. Then tell the class your reasons for your choices.

GIFTS	PEOPLE
blue jeans	a grandmother
a dozen roses	a roommate
cupcakes	a host or hostess
diamond earrings	a teenage nephew
roller skates	a newborn baby
a game of checkers	a wife
power tools	a 6-year-old child
booties	a husband

5. REPORT. Class Practice for *-ed.*

Prepare a three- to five-minute report. Tell the class about some of the things you did when you were a child. Then tell the class about some of the things you did when you were a teenager.

PARTNER 2

2b. LISTENING DISCRIMINATION AND SPEAKING. Pair Practice Words for Stop Consonants. PARTNER 2. Use this page. PARTNER 1. Turn to page 119.

DIRECTIONS: First, you are the listener. Your partner will say some words. Circle the words you hear. Ask your partner to repeat any words you do not understand. Number 1 is an example.

1. (peach)   beach   6. come   gum
2. time   dime   7. cup   cub
3. cave   gave   8. let   led
4. pace   base   9. sack   sag
5. ton   done   10. kit   kid

Now you are the speaker. Say the words to your partner. For example, you say, "Number 11 is *bear*." Repeat any words your partner does not understand.

11. bear   16. coal
12. touch   17. nap
13. coat   18. had
14. pay   19. clock
15. den   20. feed

Now compare answers with your partner.

PARTNER 2

3b. LISTENING DISCRIMINATION AND SPEAKING. Pair Practice Sentences for Stop Consonants. PARTNER 2. Use this page. PARTNER 1. Turn to page 119.

DIRECTIONS: First, you are the listener. Your partner will say some sentences. Circle the word you hear. Ask your partner to repeat any sentences you do not understand. Number 1 is an example.

1. We saw a _____ at the zoo.
   a. (pair)   b. bear
2. He seems kind of _____.
   a. tense   b. dense
3. Joe is the man in the _____.
   a. cap   b. cab
4. I bought a _____ belt.
   a. white   b. wide
5. There's a _____ in my pocket.
   a. snack   b. snag

Now you are the speaker. Say the sentences to your partner. Repeat any sentences your partner does not understand.

6. You need a PUSH to finish this job.   9. Here's a SEAT for you.
7. Do you have the DIME?   10. Don't step on that TAG.
8. Where is my ROBE?

Now compare answers with your partner.

4b. SPEAKING AND LISTENING. Pair Practice for Stop Consonants.

PARTNER 2. Use this page. PARTNER 1. Turn to page 120.

DIRECTIONS: Here are some abbreviations. Your partner will ask you what they mean. Listen carefully because the abbreviations are not in the same order as the questions. Repeat any answers your partner does not understand.

EXAMPLE:

YOUR PARTNER: What does PA mean?
YOU: It means "Pennsylvania."

ABBREVIATIONS

AK = Alaska   Ph.D. = Doctor of Philosophy   kg. = kilogram
Blvd.= Boulevard   P.O.B. = post office box

Now ask your partner about these abbreviations. Write their meanings on the lines.

EXAMPLE:

YOU: What does PL mean?
YOUR PARTNER: It means "Place."

Pl.   _Place_____

1.   Sept.   _____

2.   Tpke.   _____

3.   dept.   _____

4.   pt.   _____

5.   KS   _____

2b. LISTENING DISCRIMINATION AND SPEAKING. Pair Practice for -s.

PARTNER 2. Use this page. PARTNER 1. Turn to page 123.

DIRECTIONS: First listen to your partner's questions and answer them. Pronounce -s on plural nouns or on the verb in your answers.

EXAMPLE:

YOUR PARTNER: What makes you sad?
YOU: Tragic movies make me sad.   OR   Poverty makes me sad.

Now ask your partner the questions. For example, you say "What makes you *angry?*" Listen to and correct your partner for -s on verbs and nouns.

1.   What makes you angry?   4.   . . . thoughtful?
2.   . . . sleepy?   5.   . . . jealous?
3.   . . . happy?   6.   . . . nervous?

The Vowels /æ/, /ɛ/, and /ey/

PART ONE /æ/ and /ɛ/

In English, you find the vowel sound /æ/ at the beginning of a word or in the middle of a word.

Beginning	Middle
<u>a</u>dd	st<u>a</u>nd
<u>a</u>nswer	tr<u>a</u>ck
<u>a</u>fter	pr<u>a</u>ctice

You find the vowel sound /ɛ/ at the beginning of a word or in the middle of a word, too.

Beginning	Middle
<u>e</u>mpty	g<u>e</u>t
<u>e</u>xercise	b<u>e</u>st
<u>e</u>xcellent	l<u>e</u>sson

Contrasting the Vowels /æ/ and /ɛ/

 WARM-UP

Look at the pictures. Listen to the words and repeat them.

1. axe /æ/

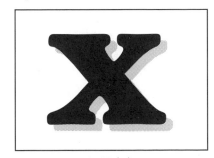

2. X /ɛ/

ARTICULATION

Look at the pictures. The heads and lips show how to make the sounds.

1. /æ/

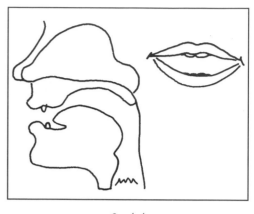

2. /ɛ/

How are the heads the same? How are the heads and lips different?

⌨ CONTRAST

Look at the pairs of words. Listen and repeat.

had–head   sat–set   man–men   gas–guess

⌨ LISTENING

Some words in English have the contrast between /æ/ and /ɛ/. Look again at the axe and X pictures on page 127. /æ/ is *number 1*. /ɛ/ is *number 2*. Listen to the following words. If you hear /æ/ as in *axe*, say "one." If you hear /ɛ/ as in X, say "two."

⌨ INTENSIVE PRACTICE

As a class, listen to and repeat the pairs of /æ/ and /ɛ/ words you hear.

⌨ PRONOUNCE WORDS

Listen to and repeat the /æ/ words you hear. Then listen to and repeat the /ɛ/ words you hear.

⌨ PRONOUNCE PHRASES

Listen to and repeat the phrases you hear.

⌨ PRONOUNCE SENTENCES

Listen to and repeat the sentences you hear.

PARTNER 1

1a. LISTENING DISCRIMINATION AND SPEAKING. Pair Practice Words for /æ/ and /ɛ/.   PARTNER 1. Use this page. PARTNER 2. Turn to page 136.

DIRECTIONS: First, you are the speaker. Say the words to your partner. You see the vowel sound before each word. For example, you say, "Number 1 is *pan*." Repeat any words your partner does not understand.

1. /æ/   pan
2. /ɛ/   met
3. /ɛ/   send
4. /æ/   gas
5. /æ/   sat

6. /æ/   than
7. /ɛ/   said
8. /æ/   tan
9. /æ/   had
10. /ɛ/   bet

Now you are the listener. Your partner will say some words. Circle the words you hear. Ask your partner to repeat any words you do not understand. Number 11 is an example.

11. (laughed)   left
12. and   end
13. man   men
14. axe   X
15. mass   mess

16. land   lend
17. dance   dense
18. band   bend
19. bag   beg
20. sad   said

Now compare answers with your partner.

PARTNER 1

2a. LISTENING DISCRIMINATION AND SPEAKING. Pair Practice Sentences for /æ/ and /ɛ/.   PARTNER 1. Use this page. PARTNER 2. Turn to page 137.

DIRECTIONS: First, you are the speaker. Say the sentences to your partner. You see the vowel sound before each sentence. Repeat any sentences your partner does not understand.

1. /æ/   Is this his BAT?
2. /ɛ/   Give it to the MEN.

3. /ɛ/   The GUESS was good.
4. /æ/   There are TAN people on the beach.

Now you are the listener. Your partner will say some sentences. Circle the word you hear. Ask your partner to repeat any sentences you do not understand. Number 5 is an example.

5. Did you _____ it?
   a. sand   b. (send)
6. I need a _____.
   a. pan   b. pen
7. Put an _____ here.
   a. axe   b. X
8. They _____ .
   a. laughed   b. left

Now compare answers with your partner.

3. SPEAKING. Pair or Group Practice for /æ/ and /ɛ/.

You see some pictures of road signs and a list of their meanings.

DIRECTIONS: Take turns asking and answering questions about the road signs, using the list of meanings.

EXAMPLE:

STUDENT 1:   What does number five mean?
STUDENT 2:   It means "Merging Traffic." What does number ten mean?
STUDENT 3:   It means "Pedestrian Crossing." What does . . .

ROAD SIGN MEANINGS

Do Not Enter 2	Rest Area 7	No Passing Zone 9
Gas 12	Signal Ahead 11	Pedestrian Crossing 10
Handicapped Crossing 4	Slippery When Wet 8	Two-Way Traffic 1
Merging Traffic 5	Stop Ahead 3	Workers Ahead 6

PARTNER 1

4a. LISTENING DISCRIMINATION AND SPEAKING. Fast Math. Pair Practice Game for /æ/ and /ɛ/.   PARTNER 1. Use this page. PARTNER 2. Turn to page 137.

DIRECTIONS: Use a watch with a second hand to play this game. You are going to give your partner some short math problems. Your partner has *ten* seconds to find an answer. That's why the game is called Fast Math. Study this example:

EXAMPLE:

3 + 10, −7, + 2, + 6. (answer: 14)

YOU: Add 3 and 10, subtract 7, add 2, then add 6. What do you get?
                        (*Wait ten seconds.*)
YOUR PARTNER: 14.
YOU: That's right! Here's the next one . . .

If your partner does not answer in ten seconds, say "Time's up." Then give your partner the next problem.

1. 7 + 7, –9, + 5, –3.   (answer: 7)
2. 1 + 11, + 4, + 8, –11.   (answer: 13)
3. 5 + 8, –6, –4, + 5.   (answer: 8)
4. 12 + 3, –9, + 6, –3.   (answer: 9)
5. 9 + 8, + 6, –11, + 8.   (answer: 20)
6. 10 + 4, + 7, –5, –9.   (answer: 7)

Now get a piece of paper and a pencil or pen. Your partner is going to give you some short math problems. You have *ten* seconds to solve each problem. Study this example:

EXAMPLE:

YOUR PARTNER: Add 10 and 5, subtract 7, add 4, then subtract 6. What do you get?
YOU: *(After 1–10 seconds.)* 6.
YOUR PARTNER: That's right! Now here's the next one . . .

If you cannot solve the problem in ten seconds, stop. Your partner is going to give you a new problem.

5. REPORT. Class Practice for /æ/ and /ɛ/.
DIRECTIONS: Choose one of these topics. Tell the class about it for 3 to 5 minutes.

a. Describe a visit to a U.S. state. What state did you visit? When did you go? Did you visit the capital? Did you go to a national park? What sites did you see? Do you want to go back there?
b. Describe the best class you have ever taken. Why did you select the class? Did you get a good grade? Would you recommend it to your classmates?

SPELLING

FIGURE IT OUT

There are many one-syllable words with the sound /æ/ or the sound /ɛ/. You can usually tell when to pronounce the vowel sound like /æ/ and when to pronounce it like /ɛ/. You can look at the spelling of the word.

Here are some /æ/ words and some /ɛ/ words. Study the spelling of these words.

/æ/		/ɛ/	
ask	flag	egg	help
add	thank	end	next
last	match	get	rest

How many vowel letters make the sound /æ/? How many make the sound /ɛ/? What letter makes the sound /æ/? What letter makes the sound /ɛ/? Write a spelling rule for each sound.

RULES FOR SPELLING /æ/ AND /ɛ/:

1. Say the sound /æ/ in a one-syllable word when the word is spelled with _____ vowel letter. The vowel letter is _____.
2. Say the sound /ɛ/ in a one-syllable word when the word is spelled with _____ vowel letter. The vowel letter is _____.

There are exceptions to these rules. Here are some one-syllable /æ/ words with two vowel letters: *laugh, dance, chance*.

There are many one-syllable /ɛ/ words with two vowel letters:

ea	*ai*	*ue*	*ay*	*ie*
head	said	guess	says	friend
read (*past*)	air	guest		
bread	hair			
wear	chair			
pear				
health				

/ɛ/ and /ey/

On page 127, you read about the sound /ɛ/ at the beginning of a word or in the middle of a word.

You find the vowel sound /ey/ at the beginning of a word, in the middle of a word, or at the end of a word.

Beginning		*Middle*		*End*	
ate	aid	place	afraid	say	gray
age	able	name	radio	day	delay

Contrasting the Vowels /ɛ/ and /ey/

WARM-UP

Look at the pictures. Listen to the words and repeat them.

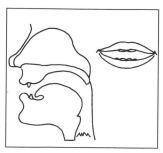

1. west /ɛ/

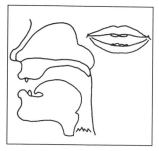

2. waste /ey/

ARTICULATION

Look at the pictures. The heads and lips show how to make the sounds.

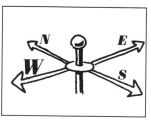

1. /ɛ/

2. /ey/ a. /ɛ/

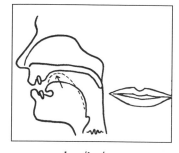

b. /iy/

How are the heads and lips the same? How are they different?

📼 CONTRAST

Look at the pairs of words. Listen and repeat.

X–aches   get–gate   test–taste   pen–pain

📼 LISTENING

Some words in English have the contrast between /ɛ/ and /ey/. Look again at the *west* and *waste* pictures on page 132. /ɛ/ is *number 1.* /ey/ is *number 2.* Listen to the following words. If you hear /ɛ/ as in *west,* say "one." If you hear /ey/ as in *waste,* say "two."

📼 INTENSIVE PRACTICE

As a class, listen to and repeat the pairs of /ɛ/ and /ey/ words you hear.

📼 PRONOUNCE WORDS

Listen to and repeat the /ɛ/ words you hear. Then listen to and repeat the /ey/ words you hear.

📼 PRONOUNCE PHRASES

Listen to and repeat the phrases you hear.

📼 PRONOUNCE SENTENCES

Listen to and repeat the sentences you hear.

PRACTICE ACTIVITIES

PARTNER 1

1a. LISTENING DISCRIMINATION AND SPEAKING. Pair Practice Words for /ɛ/ and /ey/.   PARTNER 1. Use this page. PARTNER 2. Turn to page 138.

DIRECTIONS: First, you are the speaker. Say the words to your partner. You see the vowel sound before each word. For example, you say, "Number 1 is *get.*" Repeat any words your partner does not understand.

1. /ɛ/   get
2. /ɛ/   pen
3. /ey/ age
4. /ey/ waste

5. /ey/ late
6. /ɛ/   fell
7. /ey/ wait
8. /ɛ/   chess

Now you are the listener. Your partner will say some words. Circle the words you hear. Ask your partner to repeat any words you do not understand. Number 9 is an example.

9. tell (tail)
10. led   laid
11. test taste
12. fed   fade

13. men   main
14. sell sail
15. bet   bait
16. less lace

Now compare answers with your partner.

2a. LISTENING DISCRIMINATION AND SPEAKING. Pair Practice Sentences for /ɛ/ and /ey/. PARTNER 1. Use this page. PARTNER 2. Turn to page 138.

DIRECTIONS: First, you are the speaker. Say the sentences to your partner. You see the vowel sound before each sentence. Repeat any sentences your partner does not understand.

1. /ey/   How many AGES are there?
2. /ɛ/   He LED it here.
3. /ɛ/   She's TESTING it.
4. /ey/   Let's play CHASE.

Now you are the listener. Your partner will say some sentences. Circle the word you hear. Ask your partner to repeat any sentences you do not understand. Number 5 is an example.

5. They don't want the _____.

   a. pen   b. (pain)

6. Where's the _____?

   a. west   b. waste

7. We want some _____.

   a. pepper   b. paper

8. I can't _____my boat.

   a. sell   b. sail

Now compare answers with your partner.

---

3. SPEAKING. Guided Conversation to Practice /ɛ/ and /ey/.

DIRECTIONS: Here are a list of physical problems and a list of suggestions. Take turns being Student 1 and Student 2. Pronounce /ɛ/ and /ey/ correctly.

EXAMPLE:

STUDENT 1: I'm under the weather today.
STUDENT 2: You don't look well. What's wrong?
STUDENT 1: I have an earache.
STUDENT 2: You'd better take some medicine right away.

PROBLEMS	SUGGESTIONS
a headache	take some medicine
a backache	take a rest
an earache	take some aspirin
leg pain	see a doctor
a stiff neck	
a head cold	
a chest cold	
eye strain	
an upset stomach	
chest pain	

MODEL CONVERSATION

STUDENT 1: I'm under the weather today.
STUDENT 2: You don't look well. What's wrong?
STUDENT 1: I have _____.
STUDENT 2: You'd better _____ right away.

4a. SPEAKING AND LISTENING. Pair Practice for /ɛ/ and /ey/.

PARTNER 1. Use this page. PARTNER 2. Turn to page 139.

DIRECTIONS: Here are some abbreviations. Ask your partner what they mean. Write the meanings next to the abbreviations.

EXAMPLE:

YOU: What does U<u>SA</u> mean?
YOUR PARTNER: It means "United St<u>a</u>tes of Am<u>e</u>rica."

USA   *United States of America*

1. M.A. _____

2. LA _____

3. A.S. _____

4. NJ _____

5. max. _____

Now your partner will ask you about these abbreviations. Listen carefully because the abbreviations are not in the same order as the questions. Repeat any answers your partner does not understand.

EXAMPLE:

YOUR PARTNER: What does <u>AL</u> mean?
YOU: It means "Alabama."

ABBREVIATIONS

A.A. = Associate of Arts   M.S. = Master of Science
approx. = approximately   NH = New Hampshire
ASAP = as soon as possible

SPELLING

FIGURE IT OUT

On page 131, you wrote a spelling rule for /ɛ/. There are many one-syllable words with the sound /ey/. You can usually tell when to pronounce the vowel sound like /ey/. You can look at the spelling of the word.

Here are some /ey/ words. Study the spelling of these words.

/ey/
same   gave   make   wait   paid   rain

How many vowel letters make the sound /ey/? What letters make the sound /ey/? Write a spelling rule.

Say the sound /ey/ in a one-syllable word when the word is spelled with _____ vowel letters. One vowel letter is always _____. The other vowel letters can be _____ or _____.

There are exceptions to this rule. Here are some one-syllable /ey/ words:

ay	*ea*	*ei*	*ey*
way	great	eight	they
say	break	weigh	
day		weight	
stay			
play			

PARTNER 2

1b. LISTENING DISCRIMINATION AND SPEAKING. Pair Practice Words for /æ/ and /ɛ/. PARTNER 2. Use this page. PARTNER 1. Turn to page 129.

DIRECTIONS: First, you are the listener. Your partner will say some words. Circle the words you hear. Ask your partner to repeat any words you do not understand. Number 1 is an example.

1.	(pan)	pen	6.	than	then
2.	mat	met	7.	sad	said
3.	sand	send	8.	tan	ten
4.	gas	guess	9.	had	head
5.	sat	set	10.	bat	bet

Now you are the speaker. Say the words to your partner. You see the vowel sound before each word. For example, you say, "Number 11 is *laughed*." Repeat any words your partner does not understand.

11.	/æ/	laughed	16.	/ɛ/	lend
12.	/ɛ/	end	17.	/ɛ/	dense
13.	/æ/	man	18.	/æ/	band
14.	/æ/	axe	19.	/æ/	bag
15.	/ɛ/	mess	20.	/æ/	sad

Now compare answers with your partner.

PARTNER 2

2b. LISTENING DISCRIMINATION AND SPEAKING. Pair Practice Sentences for /æ/ and /ɛ/. PARTNER 2. Use this page. PARTNER 1. Turn to page 129.

DIRECTIONS: First, you are the listener. Your partner will say some sentences. Circle the word you hear. Ask your partner to repeat any sentences you do not understand. Number 1 is an example.

1. Is this his _____?
   a. (bat)   b. bet

2. Give it to the _____.
   a. man   b. men

3. The _____ was good.
   a. gas   b. guess

4. There are _____ people on the beach.
   a. tan   b. ten

Now you are the speaker. Say the sentences to your partner. You see the vowel sound before each sentence. Repeat any sentences your partner does not understand.

5. /ɛ/   Did you SEND it?
6. /æ/   I need a PAN.

7. /ɛ/   Put an X here.
8. /æ/   They LAUGHED.

Now compare answers with your partner.

PARTNER 2

4b. LISTENING DISCRIMINATION AND SPEAKING. Fast Math. Pair Practice Game for /æ/ and /ɛ/. PARTNER 2. Use this page. PARTNER 1. Turn to page 130.

DIRECTIONS: Get a piece of paper and a pencil or pen. Your partner is going to give you some short math problems. You have *ten* seconds to solve each problem. Study this example:

EXAMPLE:

YOUR PARTNER: Add 3 and 10, subtract 7, add 2, then add 6. What do you get?
YOU: (*After 1–10 seconds.*) 14.
YOUR PARTNER: That's right! Here's the next one . . .

If you cannot solve the problem in ten seconds, stop. Your partner is going to give you a new problem. Now use a watch with a second hand to continue this game. You are going to give your partner some short math problems. Your partner has *ten* seconds to find an answer. That's why the game is called Fast Math. Study this example:

EXAMPLE:

10 + 5, −7, + 4, −6. (answer: 6)

YOU: Add 10 and 5, subtract 7, add 4, then subtract 6. What do you get?
                          (*Wait ten seconds.*)
YOUR PARTNER: 6.
YOU: That's right! Now here's the next one . . .

If your partner does not answer in ten seconds, say, "Time's up." Then give your partner the next problem.

1. 9 + 9, −7, + 4, −6. (answer: 9)
2. 4 + 12, + 6, + 4, −13. (answer: 13)
3. 7 + 10, −8, −5, + 4. (answer: 8)

4. 8 + 6 , −7, + 4, −8. (answer: 3)
5. 3 + 8, + 10, −9, + 5. (answer: 17)
6. 12 + 1, −5, + 8, −6. (answer: 10)

1b. Listening Discrimination and Speaking. Pair Practice Words for /ɛ/ and /ey/.
PARTNER 2. Use this page. PARTNER 1. Turn to page 133.

DIRECTIONS: First, you are the listener. Your partner will say some words. Circle the words you hear. Ask your partner to repeat any words you do not understand. Number 1 is an example.

1. (get)   gate
2. pen   pain
3. edge   age
4. west   waste

5. let   late
6. fell   fail
7. wet   wait
8. chess chase

Now you are the speaker. Say the words to your partner. You see the vowel sound before each word. For example, you say, "Number 9 is *tail.*" Repeat any words your partner does not understand.

9. /ey/ tail
10. /ɛ/ led
11. /ɛ/ test
12. /ɛ/ fed

13. /ey/ main
14. /ɛ/ sell
15. /ɛ/ bet
16. /ɛ/ less

Now compare answers with your partner.

2b. LISTENING DISCRIMINATION AND SPEAKING. Pair Practice Sentences for /ɛ/ and /ey/. PARTNER 2. Use this page. PARTNER 1. Turn to page 134.

DIRECTIONS: First, you are the listener. Your partner will say some sentences. Circle the word you hear. Ask your partner to repeat any sentences you do not understand. Number 1 is an example.

1. How many _____ are there?
   a. edges   b. (ages)
2. He _____ it here.
   a. led   b. laid
3. She's _____ it.
   a. testing   b. tasting
4. Let's play _____.
   a. chess   b. chase

Now you are the speaker. Say the sentences to your partner. You see the vowel sound before each sentence. Repeat any sentences your partner does not understand.

5. /ey/ They don't want the PAIN.
6. /ɛ/ Where's the WEST?

7. /ey/ We want some PAPER.
8. /ɛ/ I can't SELL my boat.

Now compare answers with your partner.

4b. SPEAKING AND LISTENING. Pair Practice for /ɛ/ and /ey/.
PARTNER 2. Use this page. PARTNER 1. Turn to page 135.

DIRECTIONS: Your partner will ask you about these abbreviations. Listen carefully because the abbreviations are not in the same order as the questions. Repeat any answers your partner does not understand.

EXAMPLE:
YOUR PARTNER: What does U<u>SA</u> mean?
YOU: It means "United St<u>a</u>tes of Am<u>e</u>rica."

ABBREVIATIONS

A.S. = Associate of Science
LA = Louisiana
M.A. = Master of Arts
max. = maximum
NJ = New Jersey

Now here are some abbreviations. Ask your partner what they mean. Write the meanings next to the abbreviations.

EXAMPLE:
YOU: What does <u>AL</u> mean?
YOUR PARTNER: It means "Alabama."

AL ___*Alabama*_____

1. NH _____

2. M.S. _____

3. A.A. _____

4. approx. _____

5. ASAP _____

PAIR PRACTICE: Partner 2